Geography Success 4

Terry Jennings

Acknowledgements

The author and publisher would like to thank Alan Ashforth-Smith for his help in the preparation of this book.

Photographic credits

Alamy/Leslie Garland p 40 (bottom right); Alan Ashforth-Smith p 59 (all); Art Directors & Trip/R Drury p 36 /BA Krohn Johansen p 12 /T Mackie p 31 (bottom); Aspect Picture Library/Tom Nebbia p 17; Sylvia Cordaiy Photo Library/Gable p 56; James Davis Worldwide pp 10 (bottom), 16, 22, 34 (bottom), 44 (top), 46 (top), 51; Eye Ubiquitous/David Cumming p 26 /Gerard Fritz p 52 (top) /Tim Hawkins p 41 /Frank Leather p 50 /I B Pickering p 28 (top) /Julia Waterlow pp 14, 15; ICCE/David Blumenkrantz p 47 /Mark Boulton p 27; Terry Jennings pp 6 (top), 7, 13, 19, 25, 30, 35, 37 (both), 38, 40 (top), 43, 46 (bottom), 58 (bottom); NHPA/Laurie Campbell p 28 (bottom); P A Photos/EPA pp 53, 54 (both), 55, 57, 58 (top); Skyscan p 33 /APS p 10 (top) /R & R Photography p 32 /Nägele Stock p 11; South American Pictures/Tony Morrison p 48 /Marion Morrison p 49; Stock Shot/Bob Kinnaird p 29; www.tografox.com/R D Battersby pp 31 (top), 39, 40 (bottom left), 44 (bottom) /L R Miles p 34 (top); Travel Ink/Tony Page p 52 (bottom); Woodfall Wild Images pp 6 (bottom), 18.

Cover photo: Earl & Nazima Kowall/Corbis

Maps

Map (p 21) reproduced from Ordnance Survey Landranger mapping with the permission of the Controller of Her Majesty's Stationery Office. © Crown copyright. Licence no. 100000249.

Maps (pp 12, 14, 16, 26, 28, 46, 48, 50, 60, 61) © GEOATLAS 1998, 1999 Graphi-Ogre

OXFORD
UNIVERSITY PRESS

Great Clarendon Street, Oxford OX2 6DP

Oxford University Press is a department of the University of Oxford. It furthers the University's objective of excellence in research, scholarship, and education by publishing worldwide in

Oxford New York

Auckland Bangkok Buenos Aires Cape Town Chennai Dar es Salaam Delhi Hong Kong Istanbul Karachi Kolkata Kuala Lumpur Madrid Melbourne Mexico City Mumbai Nairobi São Paulo Shanghai Taipei Tokyo Toronto

Oxford is a registered trade mark of Oxford University Press in the UK and certain other countries

© Terry Jennings 2002

The moral rights of the author have been asserted

Database right Oxford University Press (maker)

First published 2002

All rights reserved. No part of this publication may be reproduced, stored in a retrieval system, or transmitted, in any form or by any means, without the prior permission in writing of Oxford University Press, or as expressly permitted by law, or under terms agreed with the appropriate reprographics rights organization. Enquiries concerning reproduction outside the scope of the above should be sent to the Rights Department, Oxford University Press, at the address above.

You must not circulate this book in any other binding or cover and you must impose this same condition on any acquirer

British Library Cataloguing in Publication Data

Data available

ISBN 0 19 833846 5

10 9 8 7 6 5 4

Editorial, design and picture research by Lodestone Publishing Limited, Uckfield, East Sussex www.lodestonepublishing.com

Illustrations by Stefan Chabluk, Jeff Edwards, Hardlines, Gary Hincks, Peter Joyce, Oxford Designers & Illustrators, Pinpoint Graphics, Cathy Wood

Language and teaching consultant: Anne Mepham

Printed by Gráficas Estella, Spain

Contents

(and suggested order of teaching)

YEAR 6

Where does water come from?

Most rain or snow falls over the oceans and seas. Only 10 per cent falls on the land.

There is only a certain amount of water on the Earth, so we have to use the same water over and over again. This is possible because of the **water cycle**.

The water cycle is driven by the Sun's energy and it works because, when water is warmed, it begins to **evaporate**. When water evaporates, it turns into the invisible gas called **water vapour**.

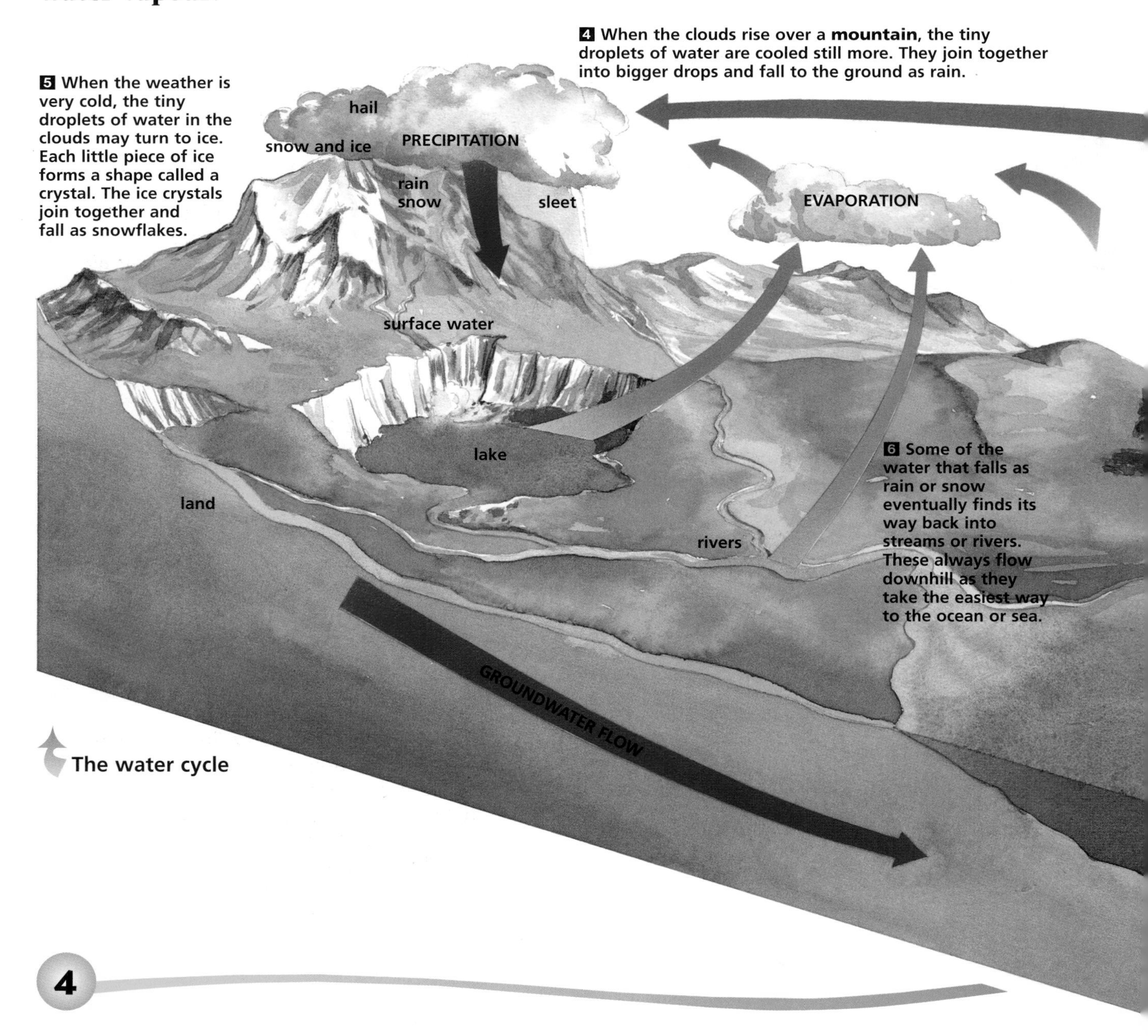

The water cycle

Water is always on the move. The water cycle produces rain and snow and allows us to use the same water over and over again.

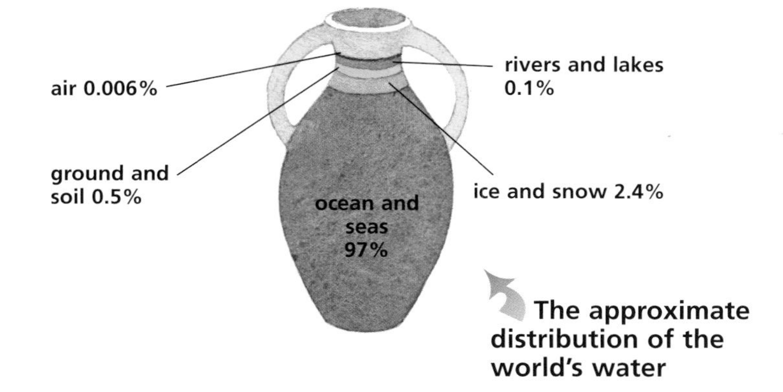

The approximate distribution of the world's water

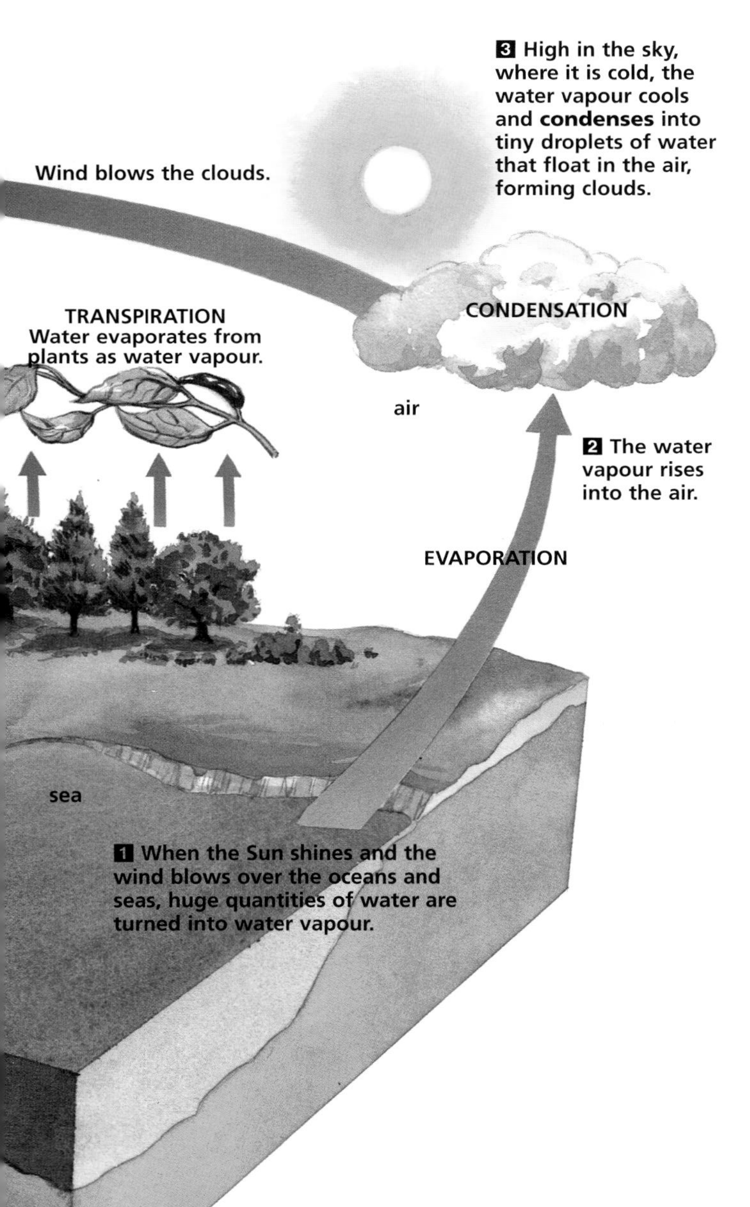

Activities

1. Answer the following questions about the water cycle:
   - **a** Where is most water stored in the water cycle?
   - **b** How does water move from the oceans and seas to the air?
   - **c** How does water move from the air to the land?
   - **d** How does water move from the land to the oceans and seas?

2. During a heavy storm there may be 1 cm of rainfall. This means that the water would fill a straight-sided tin or jar to a depth of 1 cm. In pairs, plan an experiment to find out how many litres of water would fall on 1 square metre of land during 1 cm of rainfall.
   - **a** Experiment using small containers and mark out a square metre on the ground.
   - **b** How much does this water weigh?
   - **c** Roughly how much water would fall on your playground during a 1 cm rainfall?

3. - **a** Find out how much rain falls each year where you live. How would you find out this information?
   - **b** Where are the wettest parts of your country?
   - **c** Where are the driest parts?
   - **d** Which months are wettest?

Where rivers begin

Where is your nearest river? Look at a map of your area and find its **source**. The place where a river or stream begins is called its source. Which larger river or sea does it flow into? How long is your river?

The fresh water that flows in rivers comes from rain or melted snow. When rain falls on land, or snow melts, some of the water evaporates straight back into the air, but some of it trickles over the surface of the ground. These trickles may join up to form tiny streams which flow downhill.

Springs like this often appear near the bottom of hills and mountains.

Springs and river sources

Some of the water from rain or melted snow seeps into the soil and finds its way into the rocks below. The water passes through or between **permeable** rocks until eventually it meets a layer of **impermeable** rock which will not let the water pass through it. When this happens, the water trickles out of the ground as a **spring**. Springs are the sources of many rivers and streams.

A few rivers have a lake as their source. Other rivers in high mountain areas come from the ends of melting **glaciers**. These are rivers of ice that slide slowly down from the mountains.

Near its source, a river is usually well above sea-level and flows very fast downhill. Even though it may be small, it will become larger and flow even faster after heavy rain, or when the snow on the mountains melts.

Erosion

All streams contain sand and other pieces of rock which are **transported** (carried along) by the water. The moving water and the rocky material it carries bump, rub and scrape the bottom and sides of the stream, slowly wearing them away. This is called **erosion**. The stream carves a V-shaped **valley** for itself, while the worn-away rock is carried towards the sea.

Because it flows very fast, a mountain stream can push large boulders along. The source of this stream is a glacier in the mountains of Switzerland.

A pot-hole in the bed of a dried-up river in Tunisia

Tributaries

The young river grows bigger and bigger as it is joined by other small rivers and streams. The rivers and streams that join the main one are called **tributaries**, and the area of land which supplies a river with its water is called the river **basin**. The more water the river has, and the faster the water flows, the deeper the valley it carves.

Pot-holes

While the stones and lumps of rock in the river carve away its bottom and sides, they also bump into each other. Pieces break off them and form smaller pieces of gravel, sand and mud that are swept along by the current. If a pebble gets caught in a small hollow on the river bed, it swirls around and around under the water, carving out a hole in the rock called a **pot-hole**.

Activities

1 Work with a friend. Make a list of all the rivers you can think of. Now use an atlas to see if you can find these rivers. Which ocean or sea does each river flow into?

2 After a heavy shower of rain, visit your local river or stream with a responsible adult. Is the water cloudy or clear? If the water is cloudy, carefully fill a clear plastic bottle or jar with water from the river. Stand the bottle or jar on a windowsill. Watch the materials in the water settle. What kinds of materials are they? In which order do they settle?

3 Write down all the ways in which rivers can **a** help people, **b** get in the way, and **c** be a danger to people.

4 As a river moves, it transports (carries) materials. Answer these questions about river transport:
   a Does material travel faster when the river is flowing down a steep slope or across flat land?
   b Does a river in flood transport more or less material? Why?
   c Will grains of sand or pebbles move the quickest? Why?

Down to the sea

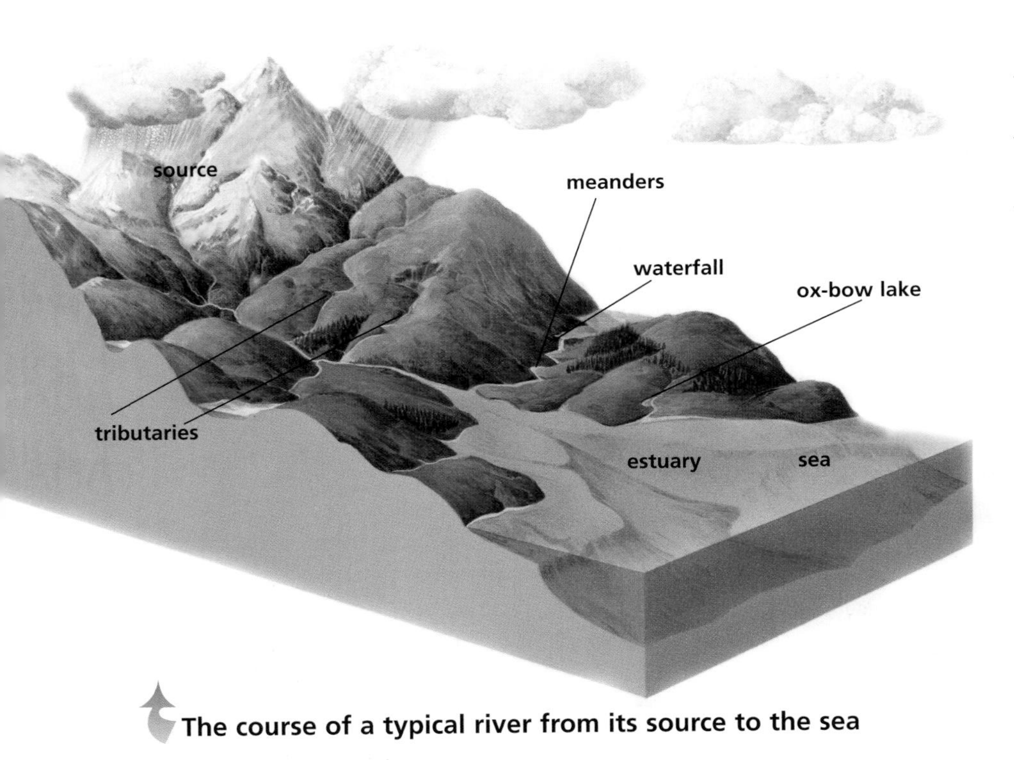

The course of a typical river from its source to the sea

How are waterfalls formed?

There are often **waterfalls** in the early stages of a river.

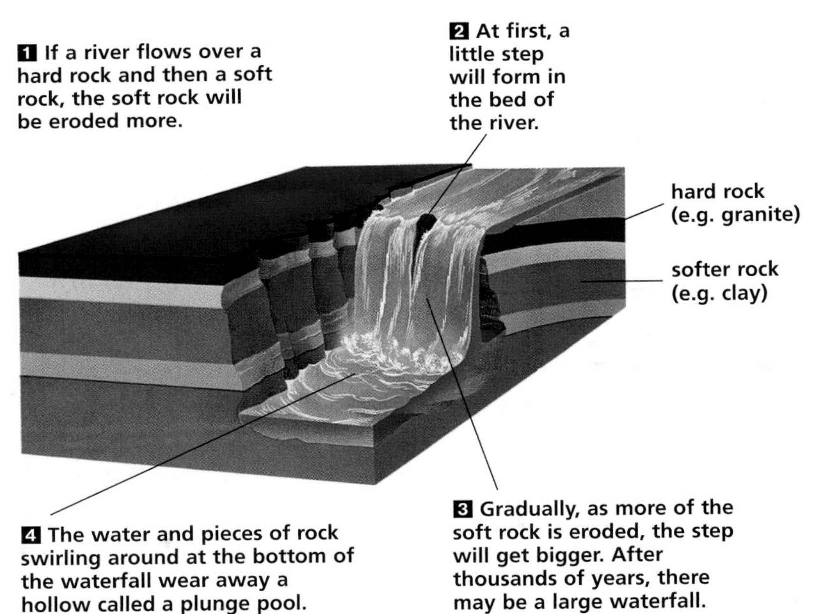

What are meanders?

When the river leaves the hills and mountains behind, the ground is less steep and the river flows more slowly. It can no longer carry boulders and large pieces of rock, but it can carry large quantities of sand, mud and small stones. The river no longer digs down so deeply into its bed, but it still moves fast enough to erode its banks and widen its valley. It makes wide S-shaped bends, called **meanders**.

Meanders are formed when the water wears away the outer bank at a bend in the river. If a car goes around a sharp bend, the passengers may be thrown to one side. When a river flows around a corner, the water and pieces of rock are thrown to the outside bank. The outside bank is worn away and a small **cliff** is formed. On the inside of the bend, the water moves more slowly. Here, some of the mud, sand and gravel sink to the river bed.

Sometimes, a river will cut off meanders from the main river. These bends form **ox-bow lakes**, which eventually dry up.

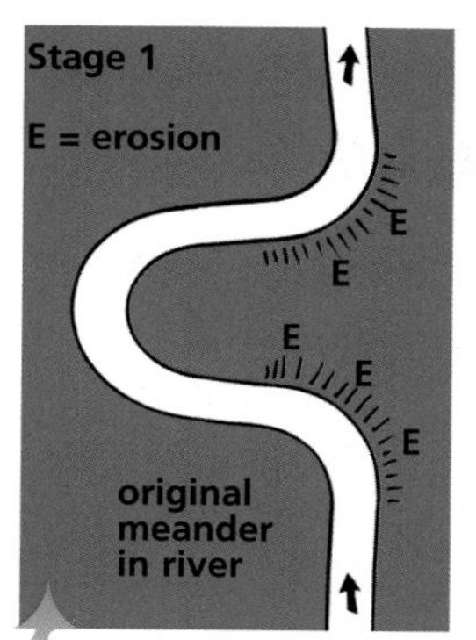

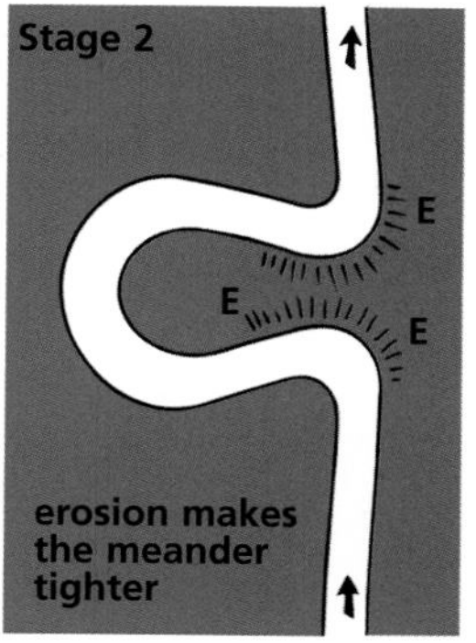

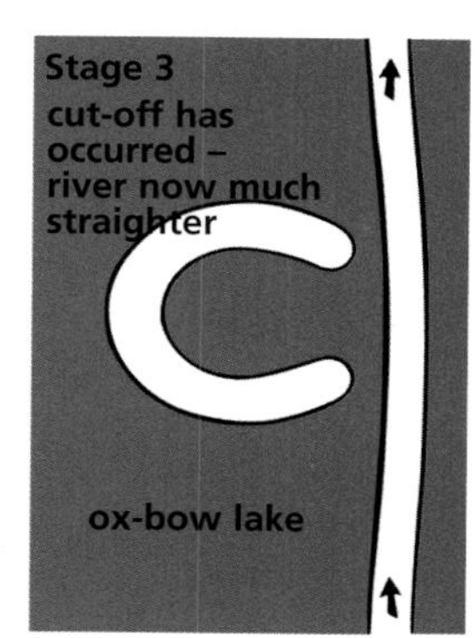

How an ox-bow lake is formed

Where is the floodplain?

As the river reaches the flat lowland, it is flowing even more slowly, and its water is now muddy from the sand and mud it is carrying. The river is no longer powerful enough to erode the land.

After heavy rain, or when the snow has melted, the river cannot hold all the water from the hills and mountains, and the flat land around it is flooded. When the floodwater has gone, the flat countryside is left covered by fine mud. When this flooding is repeated thousands of times over the lifetime of the river, the flooding and **deposition** of mud create a large, flat area called a **floodplain**. The mud will make this area become very **fertile** so crops will grow well on it.

What happens when the river meets the sea?

A few rivers flow into lakes, but most flow into the sea. When a river flows into the sea, we say it has reached its mouth. If the river has a wide mouth, this is called an **estuary**. When the river meets the sea, it drops its load of mud and sand. Some of the mud and sand is washed away by the sea, but it piles up around the mouth of the river.

The river may split up into several **channels**. The mud and sand dropped by the river form a triangular-shaped **delta**. The delta is new land, made from tiny pieces of rock brought by the river from the distant hills and mountains.

Activities

1 Use ICT to compile a fact file about different rivers of the world. Record:
- the name of the river
- the mountains where the river's source is
- the length of the river
- the ocean or sea it flows into
- the names of the towns and cities along its banks.

Choose at least two rivers from each continent, apart from Antarctica.

2 Write down the correct word for each of the descriptions below. Make a drawing of each of the features described:

a where a river reaches the sea
b where a river flows over a cliff
c where a river begins
d the area of land which supplies a river with its water
e a smaller river which joins a larger one
f a large bend in a river.

3 Use reference books or the Internet to find out more about the largest waterfalls in the world. Make a chart showing your results.

Rivers and people

Is your village, town or city built near a river? If so, do you know why it was built there? Many early towns and villages were built near rivers. The rivers stopped enemies from attacking from one side. Some villages and towns gained even more protection by being built on the insides of meanders or on islands in rivers.

Wherever the village or town was built, water from the river could be used by people and animals for drinking and it could be used to make crops grow. The soil by rivers is often fertile and moist so that crops grow well, while fish from the rivers could be used for food. Many people used rivers to travel along because the roads were poor.

The city of Durham in north-eastern England began as a walled village built on a hill inside a meander on the River Wear.

Rivers and cities

New York City started out in 1612 as a Dutch trading post on Manhattan Island at the mouth of the Hudson River.

Look at an atlas. How many of the world's greatest cities are close to rivers? Often these cities grew where the river was shallow and could be crossed on foot. Such places are called **fords**. Many towns and cities are named after these fords. Other towns and cities grew up where the first bridges were built. Large **ports** developed at the mouths of rivers where sheltered harbours could be built for ships.

Manufacturing is carried out in almost every town, but some river towns developed because of industries that grew up there. Ship-building on the River Clyde in Scotland and the River Tyne in England was largely responsible for the growth of the cities on those rivers.

Rivers often form the borders or boundaries between different countries. The River Rhine in Europe forms a border between several countries. Which are they?

Like many large ports, Bremerhaven in Germany developed from a village near the sheltered mouth of a large river. Bremerhaven, which is at the mouth of the River Weser, is Europe's largest fishing port.

Leisure

Rivers and **reservoirs** are important for leisure activities. Large numbers of people take part in activities such as:

- angling
- walking
- sailing
- bird-watching
- canoeing
- windsurfing.

Activities

1 List four important uses of Britain's rivers.

2 Write a sentence about each of these river words:
stream reservoir valley waterfall
ox-bow lake estuary delta

3 Use reference books or the Internet to find out why the River Ganges in India is sacred to the Hindus. Find out how water is used by other religions.

Land use today

Roads and railways often follow river valleys where the ground is less steep. Upland valleys provide excellent sites for **dams** and reservoirs. These can supply electricity for industrial and domestic use, while the water can be used for drinking, washing and **irrigating** fields.

Further downstream, many of the rich, deep soils, formed by thousands of years of **flooding** on the river's floodplain, are still used for farming. But the floodplain is under pressure for other uses. Because the land is flat and easy to build on, the floodplain is increasingly used for building houses, factories, and water treatment and **sewage** works. Of course, these areas are the most prone to flooding if the river overflows after heavy rain.

Around the river mouth or estuary, the wide, flat areas are important habitats and feeding grounds for wildlife. They also provide cheap land for **power stations** and factories, while the sheltered water is an excellent site for a port.

The River Rhine

Two hundred years ago, roads were poor and railways had not been invented. Rivers were often the best way for people to get about, while boats and **barges** were the only easy way to move heavy objects. Some rivers are still important highways. One of these is the River Rhine in Europe. It is the busiest river in the world, and vast quantities of **cargo** and a huge number of passengers are carried on it.

Find out more about Rotterdam in Geography Success Book 3.

Small ships and barges can travel for about 800 km from the mouth of the Rhine in the Netherlands to Basel in Switzerland, passing through Germany and France on the way. The Rhine is also linked to the other main rivers of Europe by canals, so that cargoes from the Rhine ports or overseas can be sent all over mainland Europe. Near the mouth of the Lek, one of the branches of the Rhine delta, is Rotterdam, the busiest port in the world.

River transport

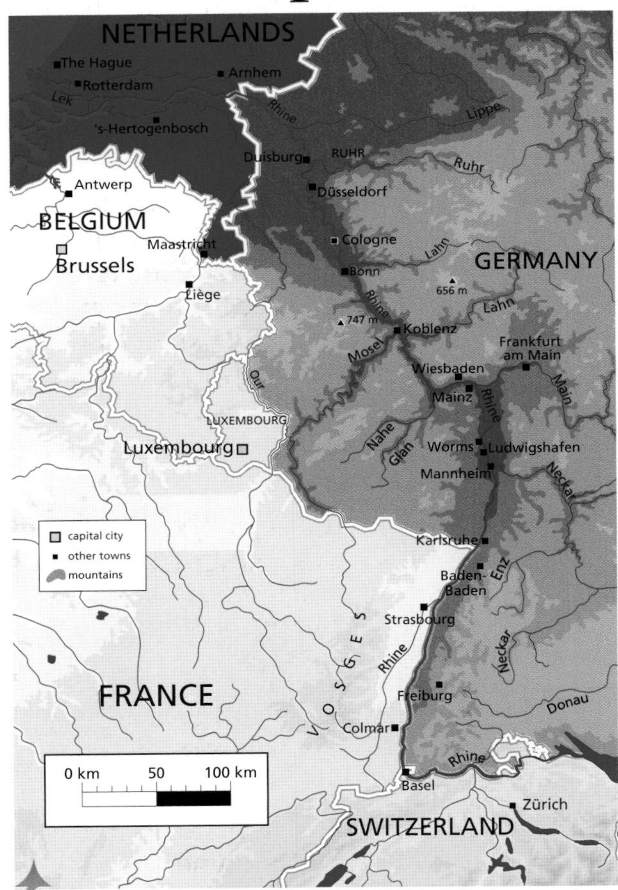

How long is the River Rhine? Which countries does it flow through? What are its main tributaries?

The port of Rotterdam handles cargoes from all parts of the world. These modern chemical barges are used on the River Rhine and along the coast.

Power and industry

The Rhine is a major source of **hydro-electric power** and there are also many factories and industrial areas along it. The largest of these is the industrial district called the Ruhr. Mines and factories in the Ruhr produce coal, iron, steel and chemicals.

As well as all the industries, no other river in the world has so many old and famous cities on its banks. Which cities are they? Millions of people live in the cities, towns and villages along the Rhine and they, and all the industries, take vast quantities of water from the river.

More than 6000 different poisonous substances have been identified in the waters of the Rhine.

One of the ships that carry tourists along the River Rhine

Pollution and flooding

Because of the many factories, power stations and human settlements, and the huge amount of shipping, the Rhine is badly **polluted**. As a result, the Rhine has been described as the '**sewer** of Europe'.

During the 1990s, record-breaking **floods** occurred along the Rhine. Thousands of people had to leave their homes and many millions of pounds worth of damage was caused. Some scientists believe the flooding may have been caused by the cutting down of forests in the **upper reaches** of the Rhine. Others blame the flooding on the straightening of the river's course to allow barges and ships to use it.

Tourism

In spite of these problems, there are still very beautiful sections of the Rhine. Many thousands of tourists visit the Rhine for holidays, to enjoy the beautiful scenery, ancient castles and historic villages, towns and cities along its course.

Activities

1 Use reference books or the Internet to compile a fact file about the River Rhine to help you with the following activities.

2 Look at the picture of the barges on the Rhine. Many people both live and work on these barges. Imagine you are a child living on one of these barges. Describe a day in your life. What would happen if you were old enough to go to school?

3 Research some of the famous cities along the Rhine. Make a poster advertising a six-day cruise along the river. Use travel brochures, reference books and the Internet to help you decide:
   a the cost of the trip
   b where overnight stops will be made
   c where sight-seeing excursions will take place.

4 Make up a quiz consisting of 10 questions about the River Rhine. Try out your quiz on a friend.

The River Nile

The River Nile is the longest river in the world. It **drains** about 3 349 000 square kilometres, roughly one-tenth of the area of Africa. Most of the people of Egypt live along the banks of the Nile.

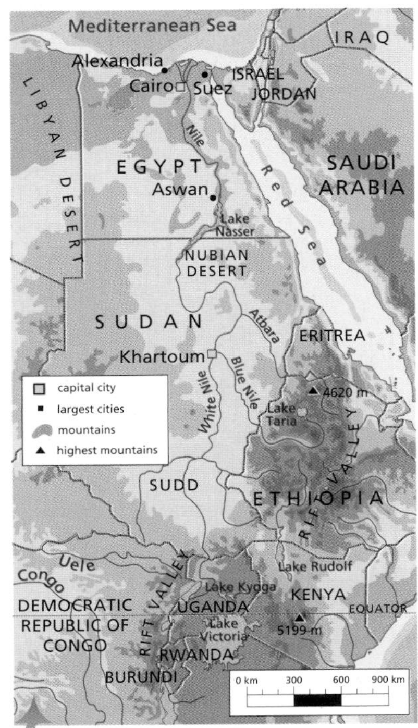

How long is the River Nile? Which countries do the Nile and its tributaries flow through?

The course of the Nile

The Nile has its source in the small African country of Burundi. It then flows through Lake Victoria and into a series of spectacular **gorges** before it spreads out in an enormous **swamp**, called the Sudd, in Sudan. From then on, the river becomes known as the White Nile and is joined by the Blue Nile and the Atbara River near Khartoum, the **capital city** of Sudan.

The Nile then wanders across its floodplain to Cairo, where it forms a huge delta, about 250 km wide, before it reaches the Mediterranean Sea. At one time, summer rains and melting snows in Ethiopia caused the Nile to flood its banks each autumn. The water and fertile mud left behind by the floods allowed the desert to be farmed along the edges of the Nile and helped thousands of farmers to make a living by growing crops on the Nile delta. Another large population of farmers works the land in the Nile's floodplain, south of its delta. All of these farmers can survive only by making careful use of the land and water. Maize, wheat, barley, rice and vegetables are important crops in Egypt, while cotton, sugar cane, dates and onions are also grown, mainly for export to other countries.

Find out more about Cairo in *Geography Success* Book 1.

The Aswan High Dam

The Aswan High Dam was completed in 1970. It is located about 960 km upstream from Cairo and it is built at a place where the river is 540 m wide.

In Egypt, sailing boats called *feluccas* (above), river steamers and cruising ships carrying tourists can sail south along the Nile as far as Aswan.

By building a number of dams, the Egyptians have controlled the flow of the Nile. The biggest dam is the Aswan High Dam. The Aswan High Dam holds the water back in a huge reservoir called Lake Nasser. The people who live along the Nile now no longer have to put up with the annual flooding of their homes and land, while small canals have been built to carry some of the water to the fields and villages. Water rushing over the dam also provides the energy to make electricity.

Unfortunately, a lot of the water in Lake Nasser evaporates in the heat from the Sun. Much of the mud, which used to be spread over the fields when the river flooded, is clogging up the reservoir. Farmers in the Nile valley now have to use chemical fertilizers on their crops. Some scientists, however, think that the soils of the delta and lower parts of the floodplain are becoming salty. This is because less water now flows down the Nile, so more salt water flows in from the Mediterranean Sea.

Settlements and transport

Most of the towns and cities in Egypt and Sudan are situated on or near the banks of the Nile. For the people who live in these towns and cities, the river is still a vital means of transporting people and goods, particularly in the flood season when road transport is difficult. Boats and small ships can travel along most of the length of the Nile, through Egypt and Sudan, except at times when the water level is very low.

Activities

1 Work with a friend. Discuss what would happen if the country of Ethiopia took all the water from the Nile so that it no longer flowed through Egypt.

2 Explain to a friend why the flooding of the River Nile in the past was useful.

3 Produce a cartoon strip to show a child's journey by boat down the River Nile from its source to the Mediterranean Sea.

4 Study holiday brochures and the Internet. What are the benefits of a cruise along the River Nile? Collect pictures of the cruise boats and details of the routes they follow. How much does the cheapest one week's Nile cruise cost?

5 Use a compass and an atlas. What is the general direction in which the River Nile flows? Can you find rivers which flow in all of the other main compass directions? Write down your results.

The Murray River

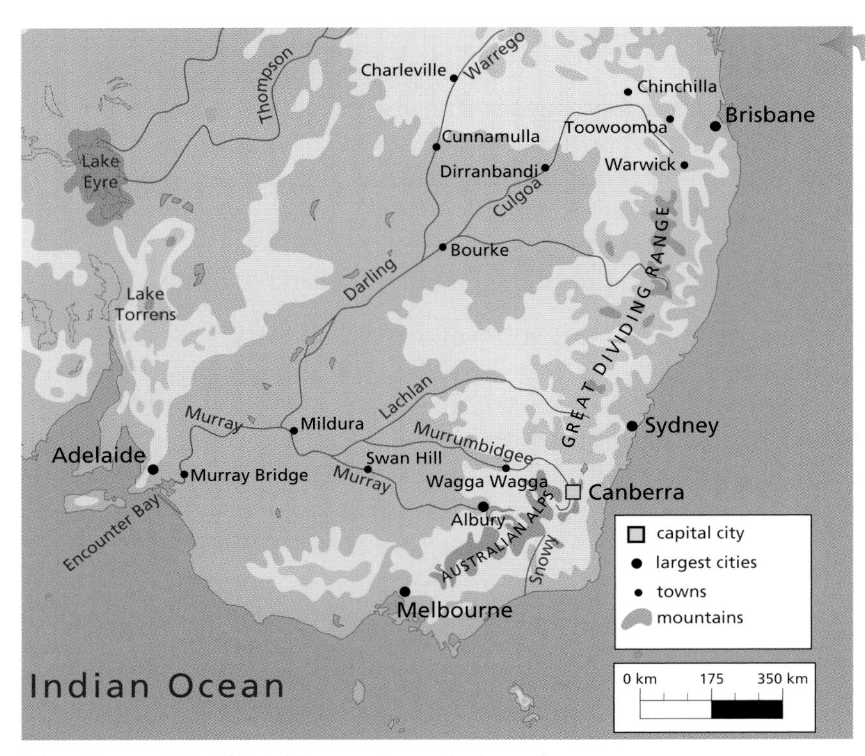

How long is the Murray River? What are its tributaries? Which towns are near the river?

The city of Adelaide receives most of its water from the Murray River.

The Great Dividing Range is a chain of mountains that runs along the eastern and south-eastern side of Australia. The highest **peaks** of this range are known as the Australian Alps and that is where the Murray River and some of its tributaries rise.

With its tributaries, the Murray is the largest river system in Australia. From the Australian Alps, where the rainfall is heavy, the Murray then flows westwards over the dry interior of Australia. Because the river flows very slowly across these vast, dry, flat areas, much of the water evaporates in the hot sunshine. In very dry summers, the river almost stops flowing. The river enters the Indian Ocean at Encounter Bay.

Drainage and flow

The Murray river system drains an area of more than 1 million square kilometres, an area nearly twice the size of France.

Comparing it with another great river, its flow is only a tiny fraction of that of the River Amazon in South America. In places, the Murray has dried up on at least three occasions.

About 2 million people live in the basin of the Murray, and 90 per cent of the population of South Australia depend wholly or partly on water from it.

The Snowy River Scheme

Many rivers, such as the Snowy River, flow down the eastern side of the Great Dividing Range towards the Pacific Ocean, but only a few rivers flow westwards into the dry interior of Australia. Many people depend upon the Murray River and its tributaries for their water supply and to irrigate their crops.

To improve the water supply to the interior of Australia, the Snowy River has been dammed. Much of its water now flows through tunnels to boost the Murray and Murrumbidgee rivers. Hydro-electric power stations have also been built near some of the dams.

Irrigation

The soils of the Murray river valley are dry but fertile. More than 400 000 hectares of land in the valley are now irrigated by water from the dams. As a result of this irrigation, sheep and cattle can now be kept on what was once desert. Grapes, oranges, grapefruit, cereals and many other crops are grown.

However, this irrigation has caused some problems. So much water has been taken from the river that its flow has been greatly reduced. Some of the water remaining in the river evaporates in the hot sunshine and the water becomes increasingly salty. At times, the city of Adelaide has received water that is not fit for drinking. In addition, some of the water used to irrigate crops also evaporates. It leaves a hard layer of salt on the surface of the soil in which it is difficult to grow crops.

These orange trees are irrigated by water from the Murray River.

Activities

1 a Find the names of five more Australian rivers. Make a table to show which oceans or seas they flow into and which large towns or cities are built by them.

b What is the name of Australia's largest lake? Where is it? Do any rivers flow into it?

2 Work with Lego, Lacey, Bauplay or some other modelling equipment. Use it to design a reservoir and dam system.

3 With a friend, take it in turns to name as many rivers as you can in 20 seconds.

4 Here are the names of some famous waterfalls and other river features. Use reference books or the Internet to find out where each one is, and write a sentence or two about it:
- Grand Canyon
- Victoria Falls
- Angel Falls
- Niagara Falls
- Trephina Gorge.

Polluted rivers

Many villages, towns and cities were built near rivers so that people could make use of the water. Unfortunately, the used water that people return to the river has often been polluted with harmful substances. The main causes of river pollution are sewage, farm chemicals, oil, litter and chemical wastes from factories.

There is so much fertilizer in the water of this river that simple water plants called algae grow rapidly. When they die and rot away, the algae use up oxygen, leaving little for other water plants and animals.

Chemicals, rubbish and sewage

Chemical wastes from factories and chemicals used on farms have polluted many rivers. Waste oil and rubbish dumped in rivers kills plants and animals and makes the water unfit for people to use. Some rivers in the world are so polluted with chemicals from factories and farms that they are said to be 'biologically dead'.

Acid rain

One of the biggest threats to many rivers is from **acid rain**. When **fuels** such as coal, oil and petrol are burned they release sulphur dioxide and other gases into the air. These gases dissolve in droplets of moisture in the **atmosphere** and eventually produce an acid rain (or acid hail or snow). This falls to the Earth, sometimes hundreds of kilometres from where the gases were first formed. Acid rain is killing fish and other wildlife in rivers and lakes in many parts of the world. Acid rain also kills trees on land, damages crops, and eats into stone buildings.

New laws

Many governments are worried about river pollution and are trying to do something about it.

- There are strict laws in many countries to make sure that rivers are not polluted.
- Factories have to clean their chemical wastes instead of dumping them straight into rivers.
- Sewage is made safe at sewage works before the waste water is returned to a river.
- There are laws to reduce the amount of air pollution given out by factories, power stations and motor vehicles. This is gradually reducing the amount of acid rain.

The workmen on this boat in China are collecting up the litter people have dropped in the river, before it can do any harm.

The River Thames

The River Thames supplies most of London's water. But by the late 1950s, the Thames was almost biologically dead. The water was so polluted that it was black in colour and it smelled strongly.

Now the Thames is much cleaner for two main reasons:

1 London's old docks have been closed down because large, modern ships could not use them. A new port has been built near the mouth of the river where it is wider and deeper.

2 New sewage works have been built, and factories have to pass their wastes to the sewage works instead of putting them straight into the river.

Now water birds, fish and other wildlife are returning to the River Thames.

Clean rivers are important because they show we are living in a healthy world. The river we pollute today may be the water we have to drink tomorrow.

Activities

You could contact environment agencies and water authorities to help you with these activities.

1 Name three places in your home where water is made dirty. Where does the dirty water go to when it leaves your home?

2 Design a poster telling people about the problems that face our rivers and what they can do to help.

3 Make a large copy of this table:

Use of rivers	Problems caused by this use	Example

Work with a friend and fill in as much of the table as you can. Remember: not all uses of a river produce pollution, but they may do.

Hills, mountains and maps

Mountains are areas of high land. Usually, high ground is called a mountain if it rises to more than 300 m above the land around it. If high ground rises less than 300 m, it is called a hill.

A map is useful to help you find your way to a place you have never been to before. It is almost essential if you are walking in the mountains. But a map is flat, so how does it show hills, mountains and the rise and fall of the land?

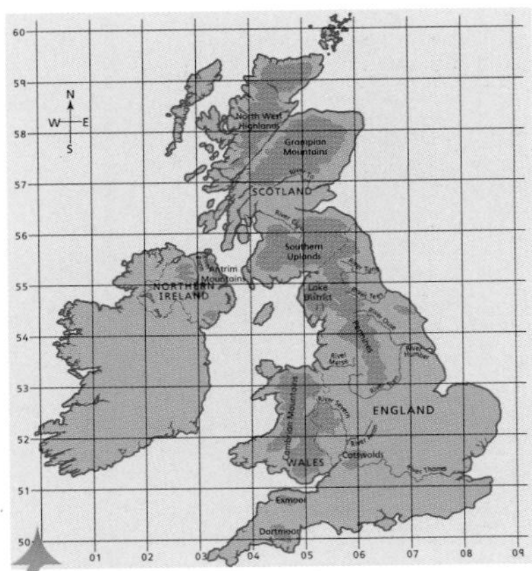

A simple relief map showing the high ground and mountain ranges in the United Kingdom

Topographic and relief maps

Many atlases contain what are called **topographic maps**. These maps show natural features of the land, such as hills, mountains, lakes and rivers, as well as things made by people, such as roads and towns. If the map shows only how high the different parts of a region, country or continent are, it is called a **relief map**.

On both topographic and relief maps, land height is shown by colours. All land areas of the same height above sea-level are given the same colour – usually shown by shades of brown or green. Such a map needs a key to show what the various colours mean.

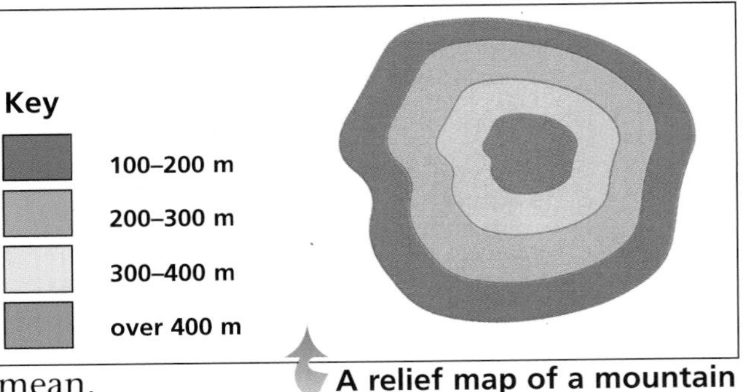

A relief map of a mountain

Contour lines

Another way that we can show heights on a map is by using **contour lines**. Contour lines are lines joining places that are the same height above sea-level. They are an important way of showing the rise and fall of the land on a map.

Contour lines are exactly level. They do not cross each other and if they seem to join up or stop it is because they have reached a **cliff** or some other vertical surface.

It is important to remember that heights (and depths) on a map are measured above and below the average level of the sea. When we say that Mount Everest, the highest mountain in the world, is 8863 m high, we mean that its height measures 8863 m above sea-level. On the British Ordnance Survey maps, all heights are measured above the average sea-level at Newlyn in Cornwall.

Map scales and contours

The differences in height, or intervals, shown by contour lines depend on the scale of the map. On a small-scale map in an atlas, the contour lines may be at intervals of 1000 m or 2000 m.

On the large-scale 'Landranger' maps produced by the British Ordnance Survey, which have a scale of 2 cm to 1 km, the contour lines are shown at 10 m intervals.

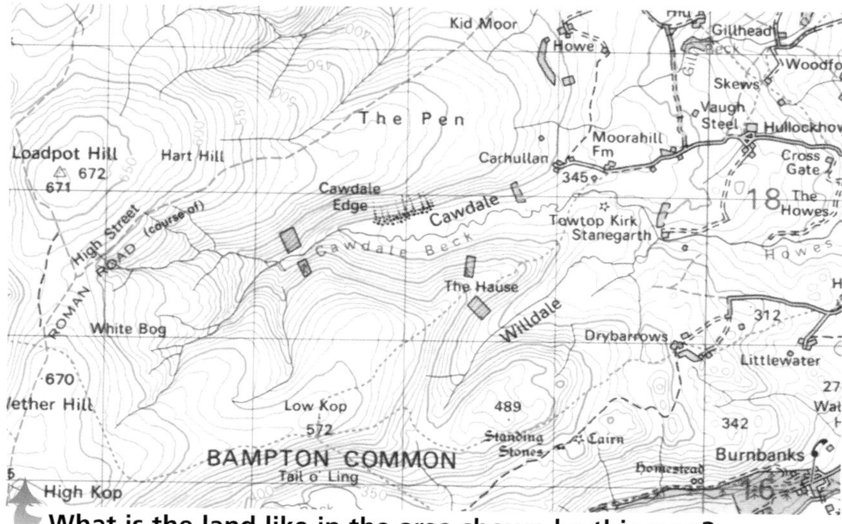

What is the land like in the area shown by this map?

Look at the Ordnance Survey map above. The contours tell us about the slope of the land. On a steep slope the contour lines are close together. On a gentle slope they are further apart, while, if there are no contour lines at all, the land is flat. Can you find the river Cawdale Beck where the contours form the shape of the letter 'V'? This shows a **valley**. The closed end of the 'V' points towards the higher land. Rivers flow from higher land to lower land, so the presence of a river helps to show the direction of a slope.

Activities

1. Study the map, above, of part of the Cumbrian Mountains in north-west England.
   a What is the height of the highest mountain on the map? What is it called?
   b Where are the steepest slopes on the map? How do you know?
2. Study a map, such as an Ordnance Survey map, of your local area.
   a Roughly how high is your school above sea-level?
   b What is the highest point on the map? Where is it?
   c Which parts of your local area are almost flat?
   d Are there any steep hills or valleys on the map?
3. Draw a map of your local area. Mark slopes on it by drawing arrows pointing downhill. Show a steep slope by using colours or extra arrows. Make a key for your map.
4. Find out how slopes are marked on roads and railways. Make drawings of the signs used and write a sentence or two about each one.

How are mountains formed?

Look at an atlas. How are mountains shown? Where are the highest mountains?

A few mountains stand alone, such as Mount Fuji in Japan, Mount Egmont in New Zealand, and Mount Kenya in Africa.

Most mountains are found in long chains called mountain **ranges**. The Pennines, the Cambrian Mountains, the Alps, the Andes and the Rockies are examples of mountain ranges. The highest range on Earth is the Himalayas in Asia.

Mount Egmont in New Zealand is a volcanic mountain.

Volcanic mountains

In order to understand how mountains are formed, we need to know what the inside of the Earth is like. The Earth is made up of layers of rock. The outside layer of rock, the one we live on, is called the Earth's **crust**. Beneath the crust is a layer called the **mantle**. Near the top of the mantle, some of the rocks have melted and are a liquid, like sticky tar. Because all the rocks around it press on the mantle, the molten rock tries to force its way out. If the molten rock does find a weak spot, it bursts through the Earth's crust, forming a **volcano**. Some mountains were made by volcanoes (picture **A**).

Find out more about volcanoes and earthquakes in *Geography Success Book 3.*

Fold mountains

The Earth's crust is made up of large pieces, called **plates**, which fit together like the pieces of a jigsaw puzzle. Some of the plates carry continents, others carry oceans. The plates move slowly, floating on the molten rocks of the mantle below. As the plates move, they push against each other, slowly pushing up the rocks in **folds** to form mountains (picture **B**).

India used to be a long way from Asia, but gradually the plate with India on it moved closer to the plate bearing Asia. The rocks in the sea between India and Asia were pushed up in folds that now form the Himalayan mountain range. That is why it is sometimes possible to find seashells near the tops of the Himalayas. Many other mountain ranges, including the Alps, Rockies and Pennines, are similar great folds of rock.

How volcanic mountains are formed

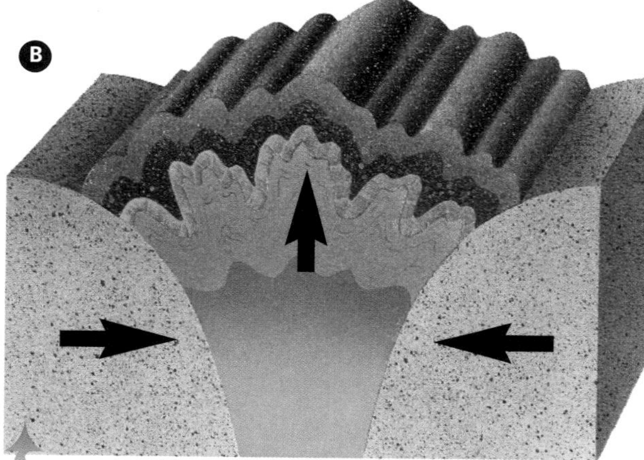

How fold mountains are formed

How block mountains are formed

Faults and block mountains

While some plates are pushing together, others are moving further apart. Europe and North America are slowly moving further apart. Each year the Atlantic Ocean is a few centimetres wider. As the rocks move, they often crack or break. These breaks are called **faults**. Sometimes, great blocks of rocks are pushed up between two faults. These blocks may be so large and high that they form mountains (picture **C**). Some of the highland areas of East Africa are **block mountains**, so are the Vosges mountains in France and the Sierra Nevada mountains in the western United States. Block mountains often have flat tops. A flat-topped highland is called a **plateau**.

Activities

1. On an outline map of the world, mark and label as many mountain ranges and solitary mountains as you can.
2. Research a mountain range. How was it formed? What is the scenery like? Who lives in the mountain range?
3. Make a collection of postage stamps which show pictures of mountains or volcanoes. Display your stamps in an album or on a wallchart. Write a sentence or two about each of the stamps, the mountains or volcanoes they show, and the countries the stamps come from.
4. Imagine that you live in a mountain area. Write a short description of what your life is like.

Mountains and the weather

As you go up a mountain, the **weather** changes. The higher you go, the colder it gets, with the temperature falling roughly 2 °C for each 300 m you climb. If you climb high enough, you will eventually reach the snow-line. Above this line it is so cold that snow covers the ground even in summer. That is why there is snow on the tops of very high mountains near the **Equator**.

Mountains are much windier than lowlands. The wind sometimes blows across the tops of high mountains at 320 km per hour.

What is a rain shadow?

Often, the upper parts of mountains are covered in clouds. Clouds are made up of tiny droplets of water. Mountains force the clouds to rise, and they may rise so high that the tiny droplets of water in them join together. The bigger drops of water may then fall as rain or snow. Often, the rain or snow falls on only one side of the mountain, the **windward** side. The other side of the mountain, the **leeward** side, which receives much less rain or snow, is said to be in a '**rain shadow**'.

west
clouds
rain
east
evaporation
rain shadow
relief rainfall
mountains
wind
sea

How a rain shadow is formed

How does the weather affect land use?

The Sun affects the sides of a mountain differently. One side may be in sunshine, the other side in shadow. Also, because cold air is heavier than warm air, cold air tends to sink into the valleys. That is why vineyards and orchards are planted partway up the lower slopes of a mountain and not in the bottom of a valley. Villages are often built on the lower slopes of a mountain, too, rather than in the colder valley bottom.

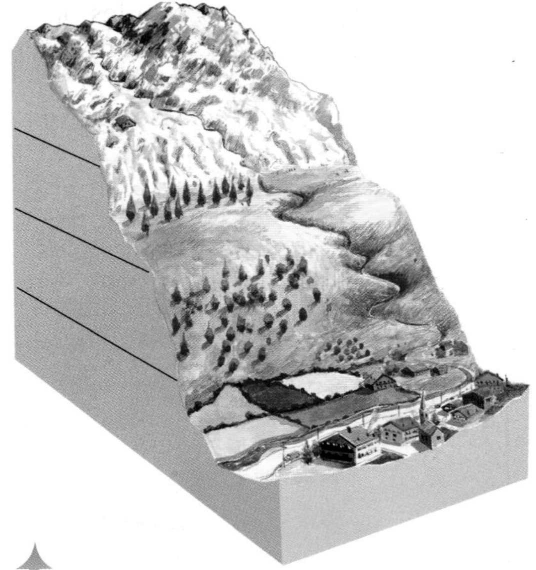

Land use in a mountain valley

Weathering

Even as mountains are being formed, they are being worn away – by the weather. This happens in several ways.

All rocks have tiny cracks in them and when rain falls or dew forms, water gets in these cracks. If it freezes, the water turns to ice and, as it does so, it expands (gets bigger). The ice presses hard against the sides of each crack, gradually weakening the rock until pieces break off and slide down the mountain.

A scree slope on a mountain in Austria

Rainwater also dissolves some rocks, such as limestone, because it is a very weak acid.

In hot, dry places, such as **deserts**, very hot days and cold nights weaken the rocks by making them expand and shrink. Slowly, the rocks break up into smaller pieces which slide down the sides of the mountain.

These processes are all examples of **weathering**. In addition, plant roots grow in cracks in rocks. As the roots grow fatter, they force open the cracks so that pieces of rock may break off. The pieces of rock formed by weathering and plant roots may form a loose bank of fragments, called **scree**, near the bottom of a mountain.

Glaciers

In some mountainous parts of the world there are rivers of ice called **glaciers**. A glacier moves very slowly along a river valley, wearing away the rocks around it. Glaciers make river valleys deeper and U-shaped.

Activities

1 a Roughly how much would the temperature fall if you climbed from sea-level to the top of Mount Everest (8863 m)?

b If the temperature where you are today fell by that amount, what would the temperature be? What would the weather be like?

2 a Find out all you can about the kinds of clothes people should wear when walking in the mountains. What kinds of shoes or boots should they wear? What else should they do to make certain they are safe?

b Find out about avalanches. Where do they occur? Are they dangerous? Why?

3 Mountains are weathered. How does weathering affect buildings, gravestones, monuments and other structures? Is the weathering of buildings in towns and cities worse than in the country? Why is this?

The Himalayas

What are the Himalayas? The Himalayas are a series of mountain ranges that curve in a great arc from Pakistan in the west to China in the east. They cover an area of nearly 600 000 square kilometres.

The Himalayas have the highest **peaks** and deepest valleys on Earth. Thirty of the mountains reach heights of more than 7300 m above sea-level. What is the name of the highest mountain in the world? How high is it?

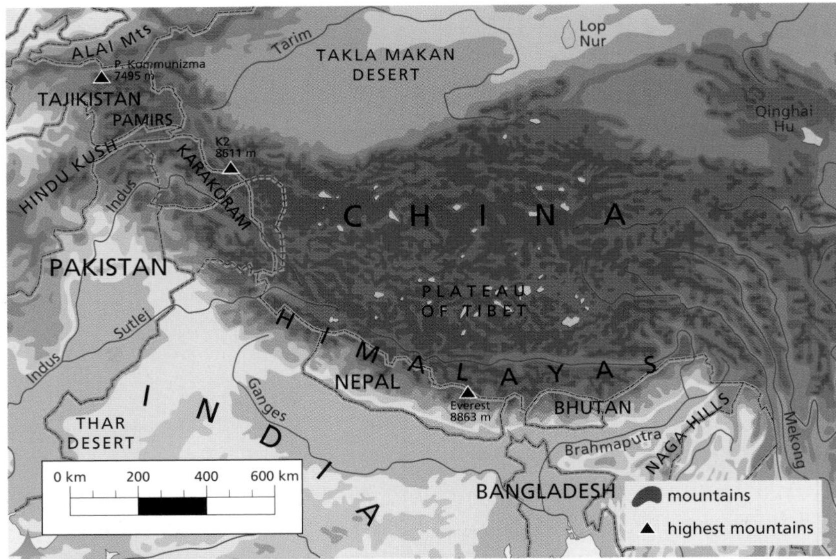

The Himalayas stretch for 25 000 km across Asia. Which are the highest mountains?

These terraces have been cut into the slopes of a valley in the Himalayas in Nepal.

Formation and features

The Himalayas are relatively young fold mountains. They began to form about 38 million years ago. Like all young mountain ranges, the Himalayas have jagged peaks. The upper parts of the Himalayas are always covered with ice and snow. Neither people nor animals can live there because the air is so 'thin'. The higher you go above sea-level, the less air there is, and high in the Himalayas the air is so thin that most climbers can breathe only with the help of bottles of oxygen.

Climate and land use

The lower slopes of the Himalayas have a milder **climate** and the soil is **fertile** and well-drained. There are orchards of fruit trees, vineyards and tea plantations. Many of the mountain slopes are cut into **terraces**, and crops like potatoes, wheat, maize, rice and sugar cane are grown on them. Sheep, goats and yaks (a kind of mountain cattle) are reared. These animals are taken up to the high pastures to feed in summer. In the autumn, they are moved back to the shelter of the valleys. Yaks are also used to carry people and heavy loads, because the high mountains make it difficult to build roads and railways and many settlements are very isolated.

The Himalayas protect India and Pakistan from cold winds blowing from the north. As the **monsoon** winds blow northwards from the Indian sub-continent, they are forced to rise over the Himalayas, dropping their rain or snow on the southern slopes. The northern slopes are in a rain shadow. In places, desert conditions exist.

Rivers and minerals

Nineteen large rivers **drain** the Himalayas, including the Indus and Brahmaputra. These rivers provide water for the people, and water and fertile **silt** for crops in India, Pakistan and Bangladesh. Many of the rivers have been **dammed** to provide **hydro-electric power**. The mountains also contain valuable minerals and gemstones, as well as iron ore and coal. However, it is difficult to mine these materials profitably because of poor **transport**.

The soil has been washed away on this Himalayan slope because trees have been removed.

Forests and flooding

About one-third of the lower slopes of the Himalayas are covered with forests, and the trees are used to make paper, matches and other products. But the Himalayas are changing. In the last 30 years or so, the population of Nepal has doubled. There is not enough food and firewood to go around and many trees have been cut down to make new fields and to provide firewood.

Normally, the tree roots act like a sponge, soaking up the heavy rain and releasing it slowly. They also hold the soil in place. Now, when it rains in the Himalayas, the rivers overflow. Disastrous **flooding** occurs in the valleys and plains below, and right across India and Bangladesh. The thin soil on the steeper slopes is washed away and occasionally even the terraces and villages are swept away. To stop these things happening, more trees are being planted, but it will be many years before the damage is repaired.

Activities

1. Imagine you have been transported to the Himalayas for the day. Write a short paragraph describing what you see, feel and hear.
2. Use reference books or the Internet to find out all you can about the mountain country of Nepal, including its climate. Make your own guidebook to Nepal.
3. What are the difficulties of living in a mountainous area like the Himalayas? Write a short paragraph describing your ideas.

The Highlands of Scotland

Which mountain ranges make up the Highlands of Scotland? These ranges contain the highest mountains in the British Isles and also long lakes called **lochs**. Which islands lie to the west?

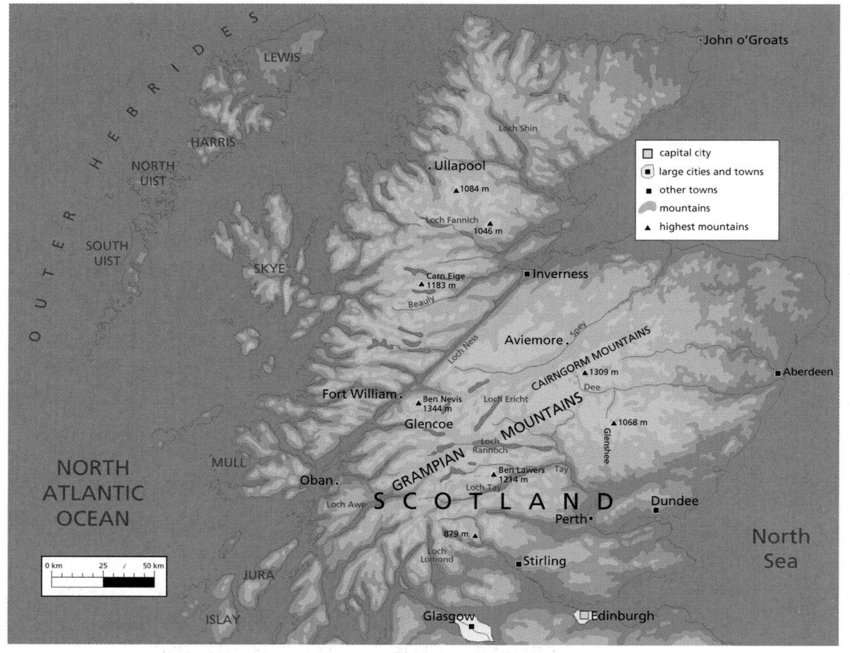

Most of the Highlands are made up of very old, hard rock. When they were formed, about 400 million years ago, the mountains were much higher, but they have been slowly worn down to rounded peaks. The soil is poor and thin and the rainfall over the Highlands is heavy, so farming is difficult and in many areas there are very few people.

Ben Nevis, which is part of the Grampian Mountains, is the highest mountain in the British Isles at 1344 m.

Farming and forestry

Sheep and cattle are kept in the Highlands. Wild deer and grouse are also found there and these are shot for sport and for their meat. Crops, such as barley, oats and potatoes, are grown in the valleys and on the coastal plains.

Most of the Highlands was once covered by forests, but most of these were cut down a long time ago. Now large areas of the uplands are covered by heather, which provides food for the sheep, deer and grouse.

When the heather bushes grow old, they are burned. Then new, young heather plants grow up in their place.

Many hillsides in the Highlands are now being planted with trees. Conifers, such as pine and spruce, are used for timber and paper. Some of the fast-flowing Highland rivers have been dammed to provide drinking water and hydro-electric power for the towns and cities.

Crofting

Many of the more remote areas of the Highlands are worked by some 17 000 **crofters**. These are people who rent small pieces of land and who combine farming and fishing with tourism, forestry or whatever part-time work might be available locally.

Gaelic was once the language spoken here, but it is now mainly used only in the north-west and in the islands. However, Gaelic place names are found in many parts of Scotland.

Tourism

Many tourists and sportspeople visit the Highlands. Why is this? There are three main ski areas: the Cairngorm range, Glenshee and Glencoe. At Aviemore in the Cairngorms, an all-the-year-round holiday centre has been built. Elsewhere in the Highlands, more hotels, hostels, caravan sites, shops and restaurants have been built to cater for the growing number of tourists, who enjoy the spectacular scenery.

Tourism is changing the way of life of many Highlanders. So, too, is the discovery of oil in the North Sea off the east coast of Scotland. The extraction, transport and refining of this oil has provided thousands of full-time jobs.

Chairlifts and ski-tows have been built to take skiers to the upper slopes.

Activities

1 Use an atlas or Ordnance Survey maps. Find four rivers which have their source in the Scottish Highlands.
   a Which sea does each of these rivers flow into?
   b What large towns or cities are built by each of these rivers?

2 Work with a friend. Discuss why you think there are no large cities in the Highlands of Scotland.

3 Imagine you live in a small farm, or croft, in the Highlands of Scotland. Write a short account of the pleasures and difficulties of your life.

4 Use reference books or the Internet to find out about the weather and climate of the Highlands. At which times of the year do most tourists visit the Highlands? Why?

Mountains and tourism

Why do many thousands of tourists visit mountain areas every year? Tourists enjoy the fresh, clean air, the beautiful scenery, or the many activities available.

What are the advantages of tourism?

- Hotels, restaurants, cafés and shops may be built and these provide jobs for local people.
- Public transport may be improved, which benefits local people as well as tourists.
- Traditional local crafts, such as weaving, knitting, wood carving and pottery, may be encouraged to produce items for sale to tourists.

What are the disadvantages of tourism?

- The influx of wealthy tourists may encourage shops and restaurants to put up their prices, so that local people may no longer be able to afford to use them.
- Tourists may bring noise and litter.
- Narrow mountain roads may be choked with cars, caravans, coaches and other traffic.
- Tourists may start fires that get out of control.
- Sewage from caravans and campsites may pollute local rivers and streams.
- Sheep and other farm livestock may be disturbed.
- It may be necessary to dig quarries to obtain materials for making new roads and buildings for tourists.

If too many people walk or cycle up a mountain path, they may kill the plants. When it rains, water will run down the path and wash away the soil and rocks, forming deep **gulleys**. The **erosion** shown here is at the top of Mount Snowdon in Wales.

What are the problems?

Many trees are removed from mountain slopes for firewood, to provide timber for buildings, or to clear space for ski runs. Once the trees have been removed from mountain slopes, there may be **avalanches** of snow in winter and mudslides or landslides at other times.

Mountain railways, cable cars, ski lifts and ski-tows can look unsightly and spoil beautiful scenery. They also allow thousands of skiers and other tourists to reach remote areas of the mountains where they can damage the fragile plant life, disturb animals and leave litter and other forms of **pollution**. Litter left by mountain-climbers is now a serious problem in the Himalayas, where, because of the severe cold, the litter may take hundreds of years to rot away.

What are national parks?

Many of the mountain areas which attract large numbers of tourists are now **national parks**. A national park is an area of land which is set aside to protect its natural beauty and wildlife. Tourists in national parks leave their vehicles where they will not spoil the scenery and they follow set paths so that they cause less disturbance to wildlife and the landscape.

Tourists in Grand Canyon National Park in the United States

Activities

1 Design a poster to warn people of the ways in which they can damage the mountains.

2 With a friend, list all the ways in which tourists to a mountain area might spend their money. Make a second list of all the jobs that tourists to a mountain area might help to create.

3 Find out about the national parks in the area where you live. Are any of them mountainous? Why were they chosen to be national parks?

Changing coastlines

Over many years, the waves on the sea change the shape of countries as they build new land in some places and wear it away in others. Waves **erode** parts of the coast and wash up the rock fragments on to the shore, forming new beaches. But even beaches are constantly changing because of the action of waves, winds and **tides**.

Longshore drift

How do waves move sand and pebbles along a beach? In places, the **prevailing wind** blows the waves towards the shore at an angle. Instead of flowing back in the direction it came from, the water from the wave goes straight back down the beach. Any sand and pebbles carried by the waves also slowly travel along the shore in this zig-zag pattern. This movement is called **longshore drift**.

How longshore drift can move pebbles along a beach

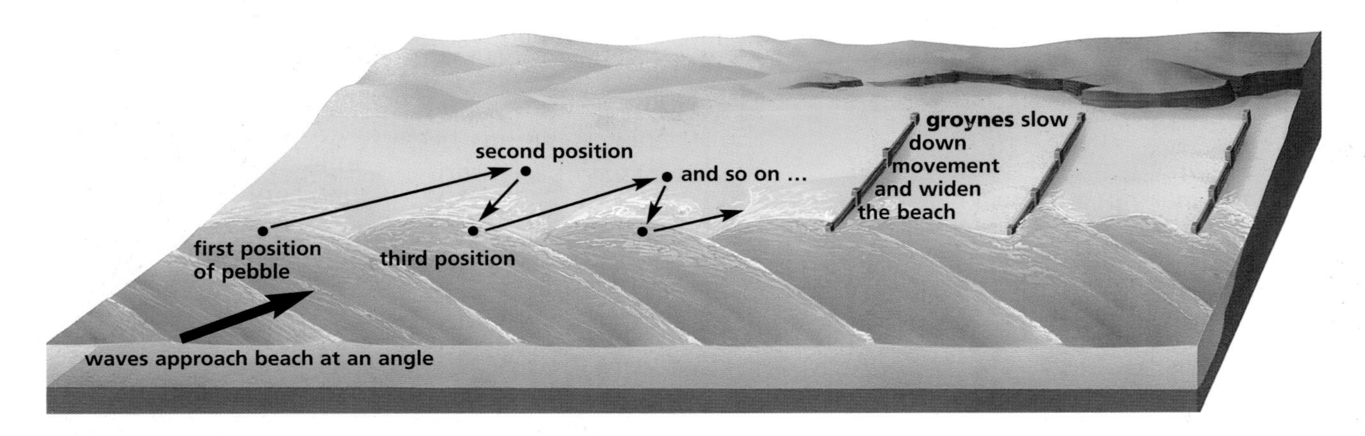

This is Spurn Head in East Yorkshire. It is a sand spit which is 5.5 km long. There are many famous spits in the British Isles, including Dawlish Warren in Devon, Hurst Castle in Hampshire and Orfordness in Suffolk.

What problems are caused by longshore drift?

Over a period of time, whole beaches can be carried away along the coast, sometimes in the space of a single year. Some holiday resorts have to pour or pump sand on to their beaches to replace the material carried away by longshore drift. Harbours can be completely blocked by the sand and shingle carried to them by longshore drift.

Deposition

When something on the coastline, such as a bay or the mouth of a river, makes the waves move more slowly, they no longer have the energy to carry sand and shingle. The waves then **deposit** (drop) the materials they were carrying.

In time, the sand and shingle dropped by the waves may pile so high that they form a ridge across the bay or river mouth. This ridge is called a spit. Sometimes a spit grows all the way across a bay. It is then called a **bar**. The shallow pool of water trapped behind the bar is called a **lagoon**.

If a spit forms across the mouth of a river, it may force the river to find a new outlet to the sea. The town of Great Yarmouth in Norfolk is actually built on a spit that once caused the River Yare to change its course.

The longest bar in Europe is Chesil Beach in Dorset which is 16 km long. It encloses a lagoon, called the Fleet.

Activities

1 Write your own explanation of the meanings of the following words:

erosion longshore drift spit bar lagoon deposition beach cliff

2 Study an Ordnance Survey map showing part of the coast of the British Isles. Draw a sketch to show what you think the coastline would look like there.

3 For the area of coastline you studied in activity 2, design an illustrated leaflet describing what features a walker or holidaymaker will see and how these features were formed.

Sand dunes and people

What happens to dry sand on a beach on a windy day? If the wind is blowing towards the land, some of the sand will be blown along and will collect behind any form of shelter, including stones, pieces of driftwood and even old shoes. Eventually, the sand piles up into small **sand dunes**.

Marram grass has a dense mesh of underground stems which bind the grains of sand together.

New land from old

As time passes, these sand dunes may blow away or they may grow bigger. As more sand heaps up on a dune, a grass called marram grass may start to grow on it.

Later, other plants, including shrubs, will grow on the dune and eventually the sand dune will form new land. Meanwhile, new dunes will form on the seaward side of the older one.

In time, perhaps over hundreds of years, if the wind mainly blows in the same direction, the wind can push the dunes inland, burying farmland and buildings. In some places, pine trees have been planted on the dunes to stop the dunes moving inland.

Once they have stopped growing and spreading, sand dunes are often used for grazing sheep, or are turned into golf courses. Many of the world's most famous golf courses are built on land that was once sand dunes.

Sand dunes at Maspalomas on the island of Gran Canaria

'Blow-outs'

Sand dunes are very fragile. If people walk through the dunes and make a new path, or if children play or dig on the dunes, they may break the thin layer of plants protecting the dunes. The next time there is a strong wind, it may blow through the gap in the plant cover and produce what is called a 'blow-out'. This is a huge hollow in the dunes.

On the bare sand in the 'blow-out', the marram grass and other plants have to start the long, slow process of **colonizing** the dunes all over again. Sometimes, where the beach is in danger of blowing away, people plant marram grass on the bare sand to stop this happening.

The largest dunes in the British Isles are at Culbin Sands on the east coast of Scotland. They reach heights of 30 m. There are spectacular sand dunes at:

- Arcachon in France
- Las Marismas in Spain
- Raabjerg Mile Dunes in Denmark
- Bodie Island on the Atlantic coast of the United States.

This 'blow-out' amongst sand dunes was caused by walkers taking a short-cut to the beach.

The importance of dunes

Sand dunes are important as homes for a number of interesting and unusual plants and animals. They are also extremely important to people because they help to stop the sea **flooding** inland.

Activities

1. Use an atlas to find out where the large sand dune systems described in this unit are located. Use reference books or the Internet to research one of these systems, and present your findings to the class.
2. Write a short story describing how a grain of sand washed up on a beach became part of a sand dune system that was eventually used as a golf course.
3. Work with a friend. Discuss how it might be possible to reduce the damage people cause to sand dunes by trampling over them.
4. Several important coastal nature reserves contain sand dunes. Use reference books, the Internet and other sources of information to find out where these nature reserves are and why they were set up.

Buildings on the coast

In some places, waves erode **cliffs** and other coastal features so fast that the lives of people can be put at risk and buildings can be made unsafe to use. When cliffs are made of soil or soft rocks, such as chalk and clay, they can erode at an alarming rate.

This house at Happisburgh, in Norfolk, is in danger of falling into the sea as the cliffs are eroded.

Dunwich, Suffolk

Situated on the coast of Suffolk, in eastern England, Dunwich is a tiny village consisting of a Victorian church, an inn, a small museum and a handful of houses. But once Dunwich was a large and prosperous port at the mouth of the River Blyth. In Norman times, it had nine churches and about 5000 inhabitants. The local people kept erosion at bay by piling up brushwood, weighted with stones, at the foot of the cliffs. But one night, in January 1326, a savage storm swept away three of the town's churches and 400 houses. About 1 million tonnes of sand and shingle were piled up across the mouth of the harbour, cutting it off from the sea and forcing the River Blyth to take a new course to the north of Dunwich.

Dunwich in the 13th century

The low cliffs in the Holderness area of East Yorkshire are eroding at the rate of about 2 m a year. Since Roman times, this coastline has been eaten back by the waves for a distance of 4 km and at least 36 villages have been swallowed up by the sea. Further north, at Scarborough in North Yorkshire, erosion of the soft cliffs caused a landslide in June 1993, during which a large hotel toppled into the sea.

Dunwich village today

With the loss of the town's trade, merchants and other local people moved away from Dunwich. Year after year, whole streets and buildings tumbled into the sea and by 1677 the waves had reached the market place. By the middle of the 18th century, most of the town had gone and, in 1919, the last of the original churches fell into the sea. After a cliff fall, human bones from one of the old graveyards may be seen on the beach. At very low tides, flint rubble and pieces of brick can be seen among the pebbles on the shore.

Land reclamation

The sea does not always win. Along parts of the Lincolnshire coast around the Wash, crops are being grown on fields that were once under the sea. This reclaimed land is protected from the sea by massive banks of clay, sand or shingle.

In the Netherlands, vast areas of farmland are actually below sea level. The Dutch people cut off sections of the **delta** of the River Rhine from the sea, using walls of brick and stone called **dykes**. They used pumps to lift the water off the land into canals. Wheat, barley, sugar beet and other crops are grown on the new, **fertile** farmlands, called **polders**.

Activities

1. Pretend that you were living at Dunwich during the 14th century. Write a newspaper report, using ICT, about the disaster that occurred at Dunwich.
2. Work with a friend. Discuss the advantages and disadvantages of building a new hotel on the cliffs at Scarborough to replace the one that fell into the sea in 1993.
3. In 2000, the Belle Tout lighthouse at Beachy Head, in Sussex, was moved back from the cliff edge. Use reference materials or the Internet to find out about this, or other buildings which have been moved.
4. Make a table showing the advantages and disadvantages of reclaiming land from the sea, as has been done in the Netherlands and in East Anglia.

On stretches of the north Norfolk coast, from Hunstanton to Cromer, cattle graze on meadows that have been reclaimed from the sea.

Using the coast

What kinds of land use are there on the coast? Besides being used for holidays and leisure, coasts also provide us with some of our food and electricity and certain **fuels** and minerals.

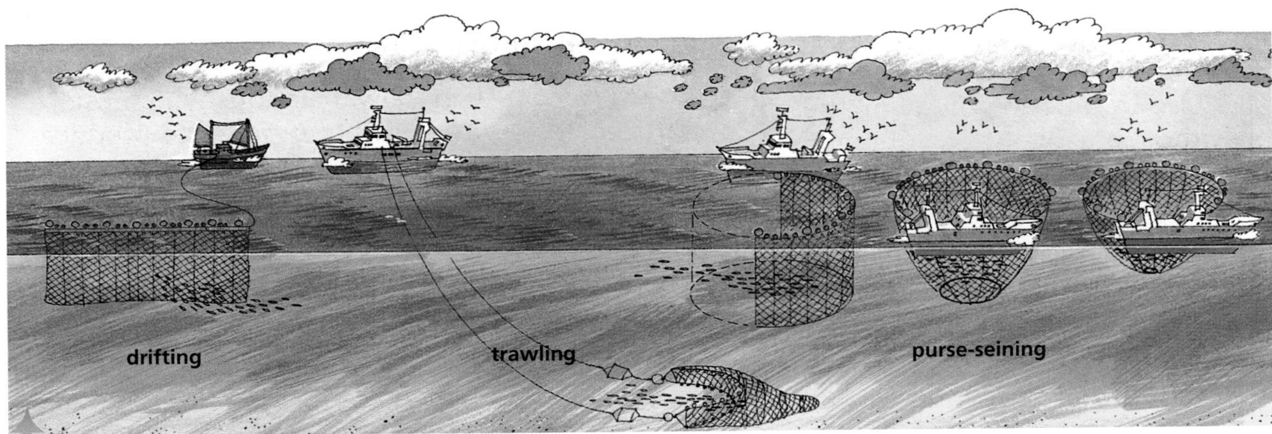

Three different ways of catching fish at sea

Fishing

Fish and shellfish are important human foods. How are they caught? Both are caught in the shallow waters near the coast. Almost every coastal village has some fishing boats which supply local needs. Fish are caught using small nets or lines with baited hooks. Shellfish, such as crabs and lobsters, are caught in baited traps on the bottom of the sea.

Most of the fish we eat comes from the deep oceans far from land. Large deep-sea fishing boats, or **trawlers**, sail from ports on the coast to catch these. The fish are caught in one of the three main types of net shown in the picture above.

Some deep-sea trawlers bring their catch back to the port to sell, but many pass their catches to 'factory ships' where the fish is processed and frozen while still at sea.

Fish farming

Fishing from boats can be dangerous, particularly in bad **weather**. In some sheltered bays, sea **lochs** and **estuaries**, certain fish are bred in special fish farms. This is done with shellfish such as crabs, lobsters, oysters, mussels and prawns, and fish such as salmon, plaice and sole.

A fish farm that rears salmon in a Norwegian fjord

Oil and gas

Much of the world's oil and **natural gas** is pumped from the rocks of the sea bed. Special platforms or rigs are used to drill wells down to the oil or gas, which is then taken ashore by pipeline or tanker ship. The oil goes to a **refinery** where it is processed into petrol, diesel oil, heating oil and other valuable fuels and materials.

Salt pans in France

Electricity

The first **power station** to use the energy of the tides to produce electricity was built in northern France. Scientists are also trying to find ways to use the energy of the waves to produce electricity.

Why are there power stations which use coal, oil, gas or **nuclear fuels** to produce electricity along the coasts of most countries? These power stations take in sea water to cool their machines and to make the steam which turns the generators that produce electricity. Coasts, being windy, are also a popular site for the wind turbines that produce electricity.

Salt

Sea water contains valuable minerals. One of the most important minerals is salt. How can we get salt from the sea? In countries with a warm **climate**, water is pumped into large, open-air ponds, called salt pans. The sea water is allowed to dry up, or **evaporate**, in the Sun, leaving the 'sea salt' behind.

Activities

1 Some people are worried because fish farming causes pollution and other problems.
   a Work in a group to find out what these problems are and what is being done to prevent them or reduce their effect.
   b Imagine that there are plans to build a fish farm on part of the coast. Discuss whether the fish farm should be built, with each member of the group taking one of the following roles:

   fish-farm owner   local resident
   fisherman
   local authority planning officer
   holidaymaker   fishmonger

2 What kinds of fish and shellfish are sold at your local fishmonger or supermarket? Where are these fish caught or packed? What are fish fingers and fish steaks made from?

3 Find out how the power of the tides is used to produce electricity. Where else, besides France, are experiments being carried out into this form of energy production?

Holding back the sea

What problems are caused along some coasts, where the sea is rapidly wearing away the land? Farmland, houses and beaches are being destroyed. In places, huge sums of money have been spent on various types of sea defences to protect the land from flooding, and from erosion by the sea.

Sea walls and reefs

Sometimes a **sea wall**, of stone or concrete, is built to protect the land. This stops waves from damaging the coast. Along some parts of the east coast of England, artificial **reefs**, consisting of long rows of boulders running parallel to the coast, are being built to protect the soft cliffs from erosion by the waves.

Large lumps of rock have been placed in front of this sea wall to break up the force of the waves.

Groynes and breakwaters

Groynes are wooden fences that run down the beach into the sea. They reduce the impact of the waves on the beach, and sand or shingle piles up on the side of the groynes facing the prevailing wind. By forming a larger beach they stop the waves from attacking the cliffs behind the beach. They also stop longshore drift from blocking small harbours.

Breakwaters are long, wide walls or barriers of rocks or concrete built out into the sea. They reduce the force of the waves before they reach the shore. They also protect boats and ships in harbours from damage during stormy weather.

Draining cliffs

Sections of cliffs made of soil, clay, chalk and other soft rocks often collapse after heavy rain. Burying pipes in the cliffs to **drain** the rainwater off them can sometimes prevent this.

Barrages

One way of preventing the sea flooding up an estuary is to construct a **barrage**. This is an artificial gateway that can be closed so that it stops very high tides or storm **surges** pushing up the estuary and flooding the surrounding area.

A different type of barrage, designed to trap water after the tide has gone out, has been built at Cardiff Bay in Wales. By keeping open a deep **channel**, it allows large boats to set sail at all states of the tide.

Managed retreat

Sea walls, artificial reefs and other coastal defences are very expensive. They also affect wildlife habitats and may simply move coastal erosion and the deposition of sand and shingle to other, unprotected, parts of the coast. Sometimes, where there are no homes, factories or other buildings to protect, it is cheaper and better to let the sea flood the land next to the coast. The flooded land becomes a salt marsh, a valuable habitat for wading birds, wildfowl and other wildlife. Just as important, the new salt marsh breaks the force of the waves and stops the sea flooding further inland. This is called 'managed retreat'.

The Thames Barrier has been built across the River Thames at Greenwich to protect London from flooding.

Activities

1 In your own words, explain the difference between a sea wall, a breakwater and a groyne.

2 Work with a group of friends. Pretend that the local council wants to allow the sea to flood a section of low-lying coast in order to protect a town a little way inland. Discuss how you would feel if you were:
  - **a** the farmer who owns the land that will be flooded
  - **b** a local wildlife expert
  - **c** a local fisherman
  - **d** the mayor of the nearby town
  - **e** a civil engineer who builds sea walls.

3 In southern England, pebbles from the coast at Budleigh Salterton in South Devon were discovered on beaches in Kent and Sussex, more than 300 km further east. Work with a friend and discuss how these pebbles might have been moved. Use an atlas and make a list of all the coastal features the pebbles would have had to pass to reach Kent or Sussex.

Threats to coastal resorts

Why are our coasts important? Our coasts are very important for tourism and leisure, while most of the fish and shellfish we eat are caught or farmed in the sea. Coasts and seas are also important wildlife habitats. For all these reasons it is essential that the coasts and seas are clean and unpolluted.

Litter can be dangerous. People can be cut by broken glass. Plastic bags, discarded fishing line, pieces of fishing net and the plastic loops that hold drinks cans can kill fish, seabirds, seals and other wildlife.

What causes pollution along coasts?

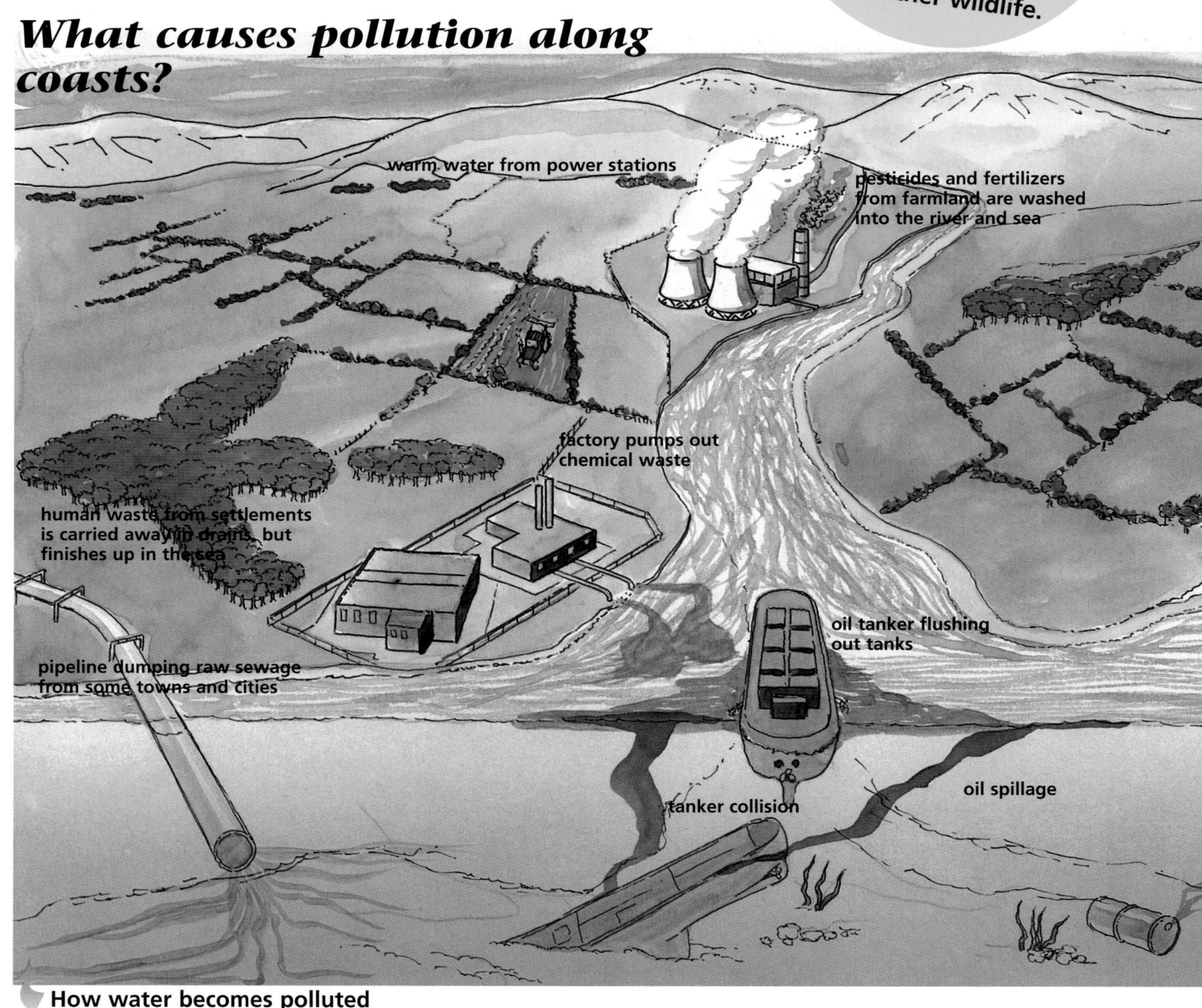

How water becomes polluted

Cleaner beaches

This beach is closed because of oil pollution from a wrecked ship. The oil can also kill sea birds, fish and other wildlife. The beach can be cleaned using chemicals, but these can also harm wildlife.

sewage washed up on shore where it spreads germs

litter on beaches left by visitors or washed ashore from ships

radioactive and toxic waste containers from hospitals and research laboratories dumped on the sea bed

Bacteria in sewage can cause fatal diseases such as cholera. They can also contaminate the shellfish that are later eaten by people.

Many countries now have strict laws to ensure that waste chemicals and sewage are made safe before they are put into the sea. There are also laws to prevent people from dropping litter, and ships from dumping waste oil. Where these laws are enforced the water and beaches are cleaner. Every year the European Union awards 'Blue Flags' to the cleanest beaches to persuade other resorts to clean up their coastline.

Activities

1. Use reference books or the Internet to find out what is done to help get rid of patches of oil floating in the sea and washed up on beaches.
   What can be done to help seabirds whose feathers have oil on them?
   Illustrate your answer with your own drawings or with pictures from newspapers and magazines.
2. The picture opposite shows the main causes of water pollution. Work with a friend. Can you think of a way that three of the causes of pollution could be reduced?
3. Use newspaper reports, the Internet and holiday brochures to find out how many European Union 'Blue Flags' each country has for its beaches. Make a 'league table' to show these, putting the country with the most 'Blue Flag' beaches at the top.

Capital cities

What is a **capital city**? What is the capital city of the United Kingdom? What is the capital city of the Netherlands?

Every country has a capital city. It is where the government of the country meets. The capital city is often the largest and most important city in a country and it has more people, shops, businesses, offices and factories than anywhere else. But this is not always so. Some countries have built their capital city specially. They include Canberra in Australia, Brasilia in Brazil and Belmopan in Belize.

The Westminster area of London and the Houses of Parliament

What is the history of London?

The Romans founded a city, which they called *Londinium*, by the River Thames in AD 43. The area is now the City of London, which is the business centre of the city. The Romans built the first London Bridge. Can you find out where it was?

Look at a map of London. Can you find the former villages of Chelsea, Highgate, Hampstead, Greenwich and Kew?

London in Roman times

In the 11th century, a royal palace and then a minster (a large and important church) were built 3 km to the west of the city. What is this area known as today? As London grew and became more crowded, and roads and railways were built, people moved to the outskirts of the city to live. What were once outlying villages and towns were swallowed up, forming a **conurbation** called Greater London. By the 1860s, London was so crowded that railways had to be built underground. The London Underground now carries millions of passengers every year.

Millions of tourists visit London every year.

Why does London need good communications?

Workers **commute** into London from many parts of England. As the capital city, London needs good **communications** with the rest of the United Kingdom and the wider world.

Five airports serve London: Heathrow, Gatwick, London City, Luton and Stansted airports. Heathrow is the world's busiest international airport. There are flights to and from about 220 places worldwide, and more than 40 million travellers use the airport each year. There are also new docks, able to handle large modern ships, at Tilbury, near the mouth of the Thames.

Almost all of the country's main railway lines and motorways, and many of its main roads, radiate out from London. Trains using the Channel Tunnel to mainland Europe start in London, and there is a direct motorway link between London and the Channel Tunnel.

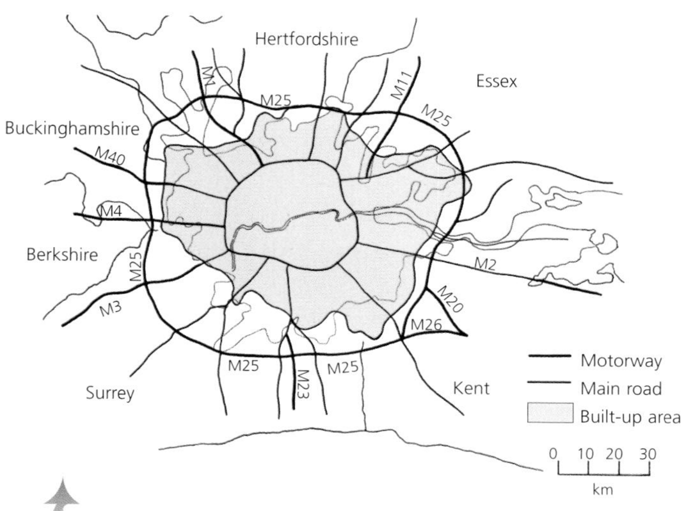

The road network around London

What is devolution?

For some people in Scotland, Wales and Northern Ireland, London is a faraway city that they rarely visit. They would rather have a city closer to them where decisions about their lives are made. For that reason, there are now parliaments, or assemblies, in Edinburgh, Cardiff and Belfast. The process of establishing these parliaments is called **devolution**.

Activities

1 Mark 10 or 12 of the world's largest cities on an outline map of the world. Are most of the cities in the Northern Hemisphere or the Southern Hemisphere? Do some continents have many more large cities than others? Which are they?

2 Use an atlas to find the names of 10 conurbations, like London.

3 Do you think towns and cities should be allowed to keep on growing? Give reasons for your answer.

4 Did the Romans settle near your home? Look for clues on a map of your local area.

5 Make a list of 10 European countries, other than the United Kingdom. Against each country, write the name of its capital city. Is the capital city always the largest city in each country?

Nairobi, Kenya

Some of the world's big cities, including London and New York, are no longer growing very quickly. But, in parts of Africa, Asia and South America, cities are growing rapidly. Look at the map of the world on page 61. Where is Kenya?

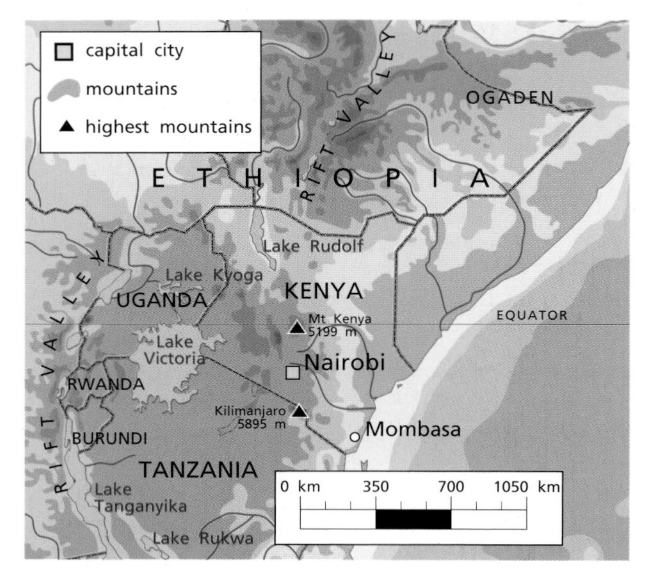

Nairobi, Kenya's capital

Although Kenya is more than twice the area of the United Kingdom, it has only about half the **population**. There are about 29 million people in Kenya, but the population is increasing by about 3 per cent a year.

Find Nairobi on the map of Kenya. Nairobi, the capital of Kenya, is one of the most modern cities in Africa. Among Nairobi's main buildings are a huge conference centre, the parliament building and city hall, the law courts, cathedral and the headquarters of the United Nations Environment Programme. There are also high-rise offices, luxurious hotels, museums, theatres, and a university and polytechnic. Like most cities, Nairobi has rush-hour crowds and traffic problems.

City Hall and high-rise offices in Nairobi

What are the main industries?

Nairobi is Kenya's main industrial centre. The railways employ most workers, but there are also light industries making tobacco products, coffee and other drinks, and processed foods. Tourism is another important industry and many tourists visit the Nairobi National Park, just south of the city.

In Nairobi National Park, tourists can see lions, gazelles, giraffes, black rhinoceroses, zebras and antelopes, as well as many kinds of reptile and bird.

Communications

Nairobi is well served by roads and railways. The main routes are to Mombasa, Kenya's main port, to the neighbouring countries of Tanzania and Uganda, and to Lake Victoria. Jomo Kenyatta Airport, 15 km to the south-west of Nairobi, is one of the main international airports in Africa.

Why are people moving to the cities?

Most people in Kenya live on farms and in villages, but the situation is changing. In 1969, only 10 per cent of the population of Kenya lived in towns and cities with more than 1000 people. Today, that figure is 29 per cent and still rising.

There is a shortage of farmland in Kenya and much of the existing farmland is given over to huge plantations, including those producing coffee and tea for export. Each year, thousands of Kenyans move from the country to Nairobi and other towns and cities. Many are hoping to work in offices, factories and hotels.

Shanty towns

There is a shortage of work in Kenya, and only about 15 per cent of the adult population has a job. Many of the Kenyans who move to Nairobi cannot find either work or a proper home. Today, several thousand Kenyans live in **shanty towns** on the outskirts of the city. Because it is 1680 m above sea level, nights can be very cold in Nairobi. Many of Nairobi's shanty-town dwellers suffer from cold and lack of good food and clean water. Nairobi city council has tried to build proper homes for them, but as one family moves out of the shanty town, two more arrive from the countryside.

A shanty town in Nairobi, where homes are made from scrap materials

Activities

1. Use reference books, travel brochures or the Internet to find out about Kenya and Nairobi. Make a fact file to help you with the following activities.
2. Make a travel poster to encourage people to visit Nairobi. What features would you advertise? Why?
3. Imagine you are trying to persuade a factory owner to build a new factory on the outskirts of a village in Kenya. List the reasons why you think it is a good idea. What might be the disadvantages of building such a factory?

Rio de Janeiro, Brazil

Look at the map of the world on page 61. Where is Brazil? Brazil is the largest country in South America and the fifth largest country in the world. It is one of the richest countries in the world, but its wealth does not benefit all the people.

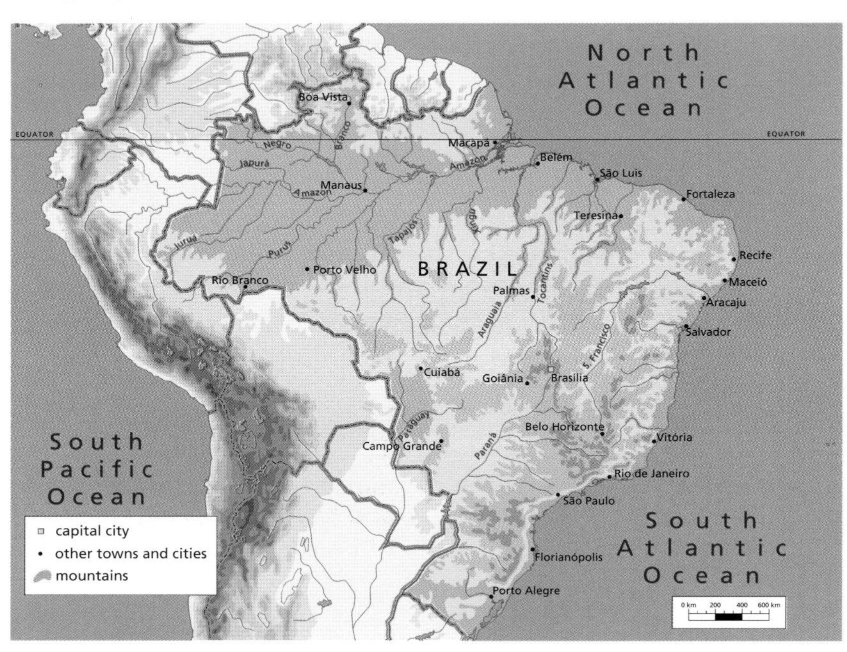

In 1950, 70 per cent of the people of Brazil lived in country areas. Today, 79 per cent now live in Rio de Janeiro and other towns and cities. Poverty is so great that 13 million homeless children live on the streets.

A typical *favela* house in Rio de Janeiro

Which are the main cities of Brazil?

Although Brazil covers a vast area, three-quarters of the people live in the cities. Look at the map. Why are most of the cities located close to the coast? Brazil's largest city is São Paulo, the second largest is Rio de Janeiro – Rio, for short.

Rio de Janeiro was the capital of Brazil until 1960, when the smaller, purpose-built city of Brasilia became the capital. The city of Rio is crowded on a narrow shelf of land around a huge bay, facing the Atlantic Ocean. The bay is lined with rocky, palm-covered islands and around it are hills and steep **mountains**, all partly covered by tropical rainforest.

Rich and poor

Like Nairobi, Rio shows sharp contrasts between rich and poor people. Wealthy people live in beachfront suburbs in tall blocks of flats and hotels, all facing the sea. Some of the beachfront houses and flats are second homes, belonging to wealthy people from other Brazilian cities and abroad.

In most of the suburbs of Rio, the streets are largely unpaved and many areas do not have a **sewage** system. On the very outskirts of the city, wherever the hills and mountains are too steep or too marshy for ordinary houses, are the shanty towns, or ***favelas***. Many of the houses here are cardboard and plastic shacks, and the occupants often suffer diseases due to dirty water, poor diet and lack of health care.

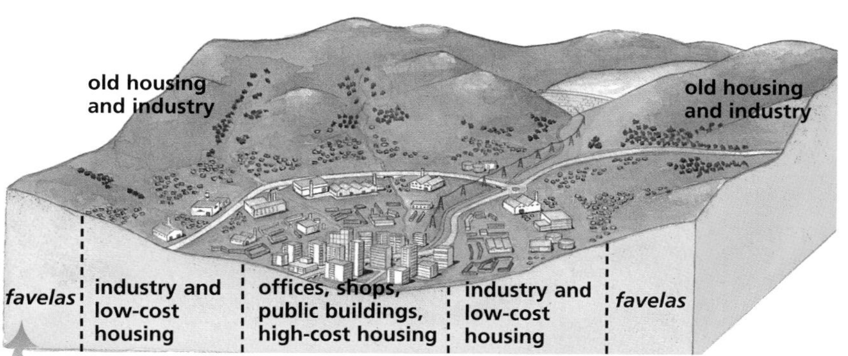

A cross-section of a typical Brazilian city, such as Rio de Janeiro

The carnival is held each year in the four days before Lent. People dress up in colourful costumes, play music, dance in the streets and have parties night and day.

In Brazil, as in many countries, most of the farmland is owned by a small number of wealthy people, while millions of poorer people have no land at all. Some of the landless people have moved to the Brazilian rainforest to clear the trees and grow food for themselves. Others move to the cities in search of work and a better life. Most of these people finish up in the *favelas*.

Commerce, industry and tourism

Rio de Janeiro is a commercial, financial and industrial centre and an important **port**. It is also a major tourist centre. Its main tourist attractions are its magnificent, white, sandy beaches, exciting nightlife and the carnival.

Rio's main industries include:
- **ship-building**
- **the manufacture of clothing**
- **furniture-making**
- **chemicals**
- **glass-making**
- **tobacco products**
- **food-processing**
- **tourism.**

Activities

1 Find out six things about Brazil from books, atlases, travel brochures, the Internet or other sources. Make a list of questions to ask your friend.

2 Copy these sentences and write True or False against each:
- **a** Brazil is a very large country.
- **b** *Favelas* are places where rich people live.
- **c** The cities in Brazil are growing quickly.
- **d** The people who live in *favelas* make their own houses.
- **e** There are farms in the centre of Rio de Janeiro.
- **f** Many people move from the countryside to Rio de Janeiro to look for jobs.

3 Imagine you are one of the homeless children living on the streets in Rio de Janeiro. Write a description of the sights, sounds and smells around you, and describe your feelings.

Tokyo, Japan

Look at the map of the world on page 61. Where is Japan? Japan is made up of about 3000 islands, which form a long chain. Which are the main islands? Most of the Japanese people live on these islands, even though much of the land is taken up by forest-covered hills and mountains. Japan's farmland is on the narrow coastal lowlands, where its major cities are also situated.

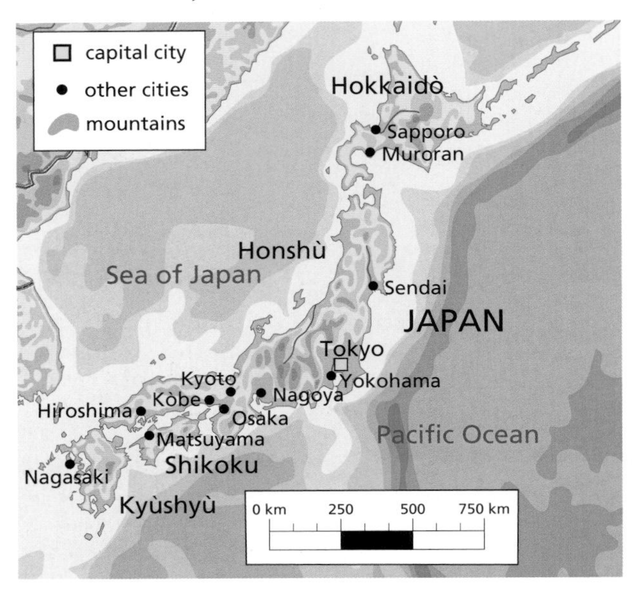

Tokyo and its site

On the map, find Tokyo, the capital of Japan. Tokyo is a wealthy city and seaport. It is one of the world's largest cities, with a population of about 8 million.

There has been a settlement at the mouth of the Sumida River since prehistoric times. Tokyo became the capital of Japan, in place of Kyoto, in 1868, and then grew rapidly. Tokyo's growth was halted twice during the 20th century. In 1923, an earthquake destroyed the city's railway network and much of the inner city, and about 143 000 people were killed. During the Second World War, American bombers destroyed much of the city, killing many thousands of people.

Business and industries

Today, government offices, the headquarters of international companies and banks, and major universities occupy the city centre. There are also national museums and theatres, department stores and shops. Modern buildings stand alongside the imperial palace and many ancient religious shrines. Thousands of factories, large and small, produce everything from computers to heavy machinery.

Before 1945, most Japanese people lived in rural villages. Today, 78 per cent of the population lives in towns and cities.

Public transport in Tokyo is fast, frequent and very crowded. Every day about 10 million workers commute into the city from the suburbs, mostly by train. In spite of the fast trains, their journey takes one to two hours.

More than a quarter of Japan's population of 124 million people live within 50 km of the centre of Tokyo.

Partly because land is so expensive and in such short supply, Tokyo is one of the most expensive cities in the world for the visitor. Prices in hotels, restaurants and places of entertainment are all very high.

Land use and communications

Much of the land on which Tokyo stands has been reclaimed from the sea. The high cost of land and small amount of space available has also led to the steady expansion of Tokyo into the suburbs. The city now has 26 satellite cities.

Cities compared

Tokyo and the three other cities described in this section are like all cities in some ways. What do they have in common?

- They all have offices, shops and public buildings in the centre.
- They all have areas with good houses and areas with poorer houses.
- They all get bigger by growing out from the centre.
- Most people in cities now live away from the centre.

Activities

1 Use reference books or the Internet to find out about Japan and Tokyo. Make a fact file to help with the following activities.

2 Pretend you have been transported to Tokyo for the day. Write a description of what you see, feel, hear and smell. What do you eat? Are you sad or pleased to leave at the end of the day?

3 **a** Make a list of Japanese companies and some of the goods they make.
b What do you have at home that was made in Japan?

4 Describe the similarities and differences between Tokyo and a city you know. Find a way to display your comparisons.

5 Look at the map of Japan opposite. Measure the approximate distances between the places listed below:
a Tokyo and Sapporo
b Tokyo and Kyoto
c Tokyo and Nagasaki
d Tokyo and Nagoya.

Food and us

Never before have we had so wide a choice, or so regular a supply, of good food. Refrigeration, canning, freeze-drying, worldwide trade and fast **transport** have given people in **developed countries** a wide variety of foods all the year round. The banana in your lunch box may have come from Africa or the Caribbean, the cheese in your sandwich from New Zealand. The white rice you eat may have come from India or the United States, and the pasta from Italy, while your breakfast cereals may have come from Canada.

Your body needs a variety of foods and a balanced diet if it is to grow and stay healthy. Unfortunately, not everyone gets the foods that they need in the right quantities.

During your lifetime you will probably eat 50 tonnes of food, and drink about 50 000 litres of liquid.

For people in developed countries, there is a huge range of foods available.

Too much of a good thing

In developed countries, doctors are worried by the effects of people eating too much of some kinds of food. People who overeat and do not exercise may become **obese**, or seriously overweight. Obese people have a greater risk of tooth decay, heart attacks, strokes, diabetes and certain forms of cancer. Doctors often call complaints that result from overeating 'diseases of **affluence**'.

In the United States, 33 per cent of adults are obese. In the United Kingdom, 20 per cent are obese.

Some people have too much to eat!

Worldwide, the number of overweight people is believed to total 600 million. The chart below shows the percentage of people in various countries who are overweight. The United States and United Kingdom are developed countries. China, India and Ethiopia are less developed, poorer countries.

Country	Percentage of people who are overweight
United States	55
United Kingdom	51
China	7
India	7
Ethiopia	2

Not everyone has enough to eat.

Hunger

Do you ever feel hungry? Do you ever think you can't wait for the next meal? Do you ever say, 'I'm starving!'? What do you do to satisfy your hunger? You probably only have to go to the larder, the refrigerator or the local food shop.

Now, imagine you haven't eaten properly for days, weeks, or even months. Because you are so hungry you have been forced to eat tree leaves or bark. The food that is available is so expensive you cannot afford to buy it. How would you feel?

What would happen to your body? You would become weaker day by day. As your muscles wither, you would begin to look like a framework of skin and bone. If you were not able to get food soon, you would probably die of starvation or disease.

Are you beginning to have some idea of what it would be like to live in a place where there is a **famine**? A famine is a severe shortage of food that generally affects a large number of people over a wide area. Such a famine may go on for many months, or even years.

Activities

1 Make a list of the foods you have eaten today. Which countries did each of the foods come from? Display this information on an outline map of the world.

2 Choose one of the main food crops, such as wheat, rice or potatoes. Use reference books or the Internet to find out where, when and how the crop is grown and harvested. How does your chosen crop plant get to the shops and supermarkets? What kinds of meals is it used for?

3 Obtain a map of your local area. Mark on it where the nearest food shops and supermarkets are situated. What is the shortest distance you would have to walk **a** from your home, **b** from your school, to buy food?

How does hunger affect people?

While many people in developed countries have too much food, every night 500 million children and 300 million adults in the world go to bed hungry. Every morning they wake up to face another day without proper food. There are more poorly fed children in the world today than ever before.

Each year over 12 million children die from hunger-related diseases in poorer countries: that is 33 000 children every single day.

A malnourished baby being fed in Sudan in 1998

What is malnourishment?

People who do not get enough of the right food are said to be **malnourished**. They do not have a balanced diet to keep their bodies fit and strong. Malnourished children grow more slowly than well-fed children and they fall ill more easily from illnesses such as diarrhoea and measles.

During a famine, adults become too weak to work properly and they cannot farm the land. If grain stores are used for food, there will be no seed to plant the next year and so there will be no harvest. Those people who have some form of transport, or who are strong enough to walk, may leave the area, hoping to find some place where there is food. They may never return, and so families and communities break down. Younger adults usually recover from a period of famine. Children, on the other hand, may suffer permanent mental and physical damage, while babies and old people often die.

Women and children during a famine in Somalia in 2000

Famines in history

There is nothing new about famine. Severe shortages of food have occurred since ancient times. There have been more than 400 major famines during recorded history. Famines happened in Ancient Egypt, and during the Middle Ages the British Isles suffered at least 95 famines. The potato famine in Ireland in the 1840s, caused by potato blight, a fungus disease, led to about 1 100 000 people dying of starvation and famine-related diseases. Up to 1.5 million more people emigrated to North America and mainland Britain to escape the famine.

Refugees from Eritrea, suffering from famine, in a camp in Sudan in 2000

Some of the worst famines have occurred in Asia. It is estimated that 10 million people died during a famine in India between 1769 and 1770. A similar number of people died in a famine in northern China in 1877 and 1878.

Famine myths

Many people believe that we have famines because there is simply not enough food to go round, or because there are too many people. The reality is that there is more than enough food for everyone in the world. The problem is that not enough food reaches the people who most need it. In other words, we do not need to produce more food, but simply to share it out more fairly. Up to a quarter of all the food available in North American supermarkets goes rotten or is thrown away, while, in the United Kingdom, supermarkets and shops throw away food worth more than £350 million every year.

Most pet dogs in developed countries have a better diet than millions of children in poorer, developing countries.

Activities

1 Collect news cuttings of famines. Mark where they occur on a wall map of the world. What is the cause of each of the famines you have read about?

2 Most foods we buy in packets and other containers have a 'Sell By' date printed on them. If the foods are not sold by that date, they are thrown away. Work with a friend.

a Discuss whether you think a 'Sell By' date is a good thing or a bad thing.

b What do you think should be done with the food which is past its 'Sell By' date? Say why.

3 Write a short description of a time when you felt very hungry.

Why do famines occur?

There are many causes of famine. Natural causes include:

- long periods of dry **weather**, or **drought**
- **floods**
- earthquakes and **volcanoes**
- plagues of insects or plant diseases.

All of these things can destroy crops and animals or reduce the amount of food available. They can often be the 'last straw' for people who have to grow their own food and who live a hand-to-mouth existence. Of these natural causes of famine, the most common are drought and flooding.

This camel was a victim of drought in the Sahel region of Africa. Can you find the Sahel in an atlas?

This map shows the areas of the world that regularly suffer from drought. Can you name the countries that are in the drought areas?

Drought

What is a drought? A drought is a period of exceptionally dry weather. Crops and animals need water to grow but, during a drought, the ground becomes dry, dusty and cracked, so plants begin to shrivel and die. Soon the wells, rivers and **reservoirs** dry up too.

In poorer countries, many people grow their own food. Rainwater is essential for their crops. If the rains fail to arrive, crops do not grow and farm animals die. The price of food in the shops rises and people have to pay more money for less food. They may have to sell all their possessions to pay for food until they can no longer afford to eat.

Floods

Floods destroy crops by swamping them with water or burying them in mud. Similarly, in severe flooding, many farm animals may be drowned. Floods like this occur fairly regularly in the country of Bangladesh.

Most of Bangladesh lies on the **delta** at the mouths of the rivers Brahmaputra and Ganges. This flat **floodplain** is one of the largest in the world. The two great rivers often flood the delta, leaving a layer of **fertile** mud over the fields.

When the **monsoon** rains fall, up to three crops of rice are grown here in a year. If the monsoon rains fail to arrive, there is a drought and food is in short supply. If the rains are very heavy, the flooding is severe. Buildings, power supplies and roads are damaged, making it difficult to rescue people or to get food to those who need it.

During 2000, and again in 2001, there was serious flooding in the African country of Mozambique. As well as causing damage to roads and buildings, and many deaths, the floods destroyed crops, leading to a famine.

Famine in poorer countries

If crops fail in poorer countries, their governments usually do not have the money to buy food from other countries. If floods destroy homes, crops and livestock, most of the people cannot afford to replace the things they have lost.

Poorer countries find it very difficult to recover from famine. Many rely on help from international organizations, such as Oxfam and Save the Children.

This family, stranded during the floods in Mozambique, waits for rescue.

Activities

1. Use reference books and the Internet to help you make a time-line showing major famines across the world. Show where each famine occurred and how many people are believed to have died.
2. Many organizations are working to try to help famine victims. They include the Red Cross and Red Crescent, OXFAM, Save the Children, UNICEF, ACTIONAID, Christian Aid and CAFOD. Choose one of these organizations and find out where in the world it is supporting famine victims and what it is doing to help them.
3. Imagine you are working in Africa on the edge of the Sahara Desert, helping famine victims. Write a letter to a friend describing what you see around you and explaining why life is so hard. Give at least four reasons.

Famines caused by people

People can also cause famines. Human causes include:

- wars, **sieges**, riots and deliberately destroying crops
- accidentally turning land into **desert**, a process known as **desertification**
- failing to provide a cheap and efficient means of getting food from one part of a poorer country to another.

Poverty in some countries means that people have to give up their best land to grow **cash crops**, such as coffee, cocoa and bananas, for richer countries, instead of growing food for themselves.

These refugees were escaping to Albania from Kosovo, Yugoslavia, in 1999.

How does war cause famine?

War turns fields into battle grounds, so farmers in a war zone cannot plant their seeds, harvest their crops or feed and look after their animals. Sometimes soldiers will deliberately kill farm animals or crops and destroy food stores to weaken opposing forces. Wars also prevent the distribution of food.

War frequently forces large numbers of **refugees**, hoping to escape the fighting, to gather in one small area. This puts a huge strain on food supplies. Even when the war is over, people may not be able to farm their fields because of land-mines.

Desertification

Over the years, vast areas of land have been turned into desert. This is because:

- too many domestic animals eat and trample on the grass so that there is just bare ground where grass and other crops will not grow;
- people have cut down shrubs and trees that provide shelter, and their roots no longer bind the soil together;
- where there are too many people and not enough water, the people starve as soon as there is a drought because nothing grows and the animals die.

Since the 1970s, the Sahara Desert (left) and the Thar Desert in India have become larger, because of overgrazing and the removal of trees.

International aid

Some countries help to supply food to a country where there is a famine. The photos show how food was distributed to people in Ethiopia, Africa, during a famine.

Where roads and other **communications** are poor, the sacks are dropped from aeroplanes into isolated areas.

Food from **donor** countries is packed into sacks, ready to be loaded onto special trucks and aeroplanes.

Local people sort and collect the food that has been dropped from an aeroplane.

Activities

1 Did you know that the countries of the world can be divided into the developed North and the poorer, less-developed South?

Developed	Less-developed
Europe	Rest of Asia
Russia	Africa
Japan	South America
North America	
Australia	
New Zealand	

Draw a map to show where the developed and less-developed parts of the world are.

2 Collect newspaper reports about wars and other armed conflicts around the world. Listen to radio and television news bulletins. On a map of the world, mark the countries where wars and other armed conflicts are taking place. Are these countries in the developed North or the poorer South?

3 Collect food labels, packets and wrappings. Where were the foods grown or manufactured? How many of the foods came from the poorer countries of the 'South'? Discuss with a friend whether you think this is a good thing or a bad thing.

The British Isles

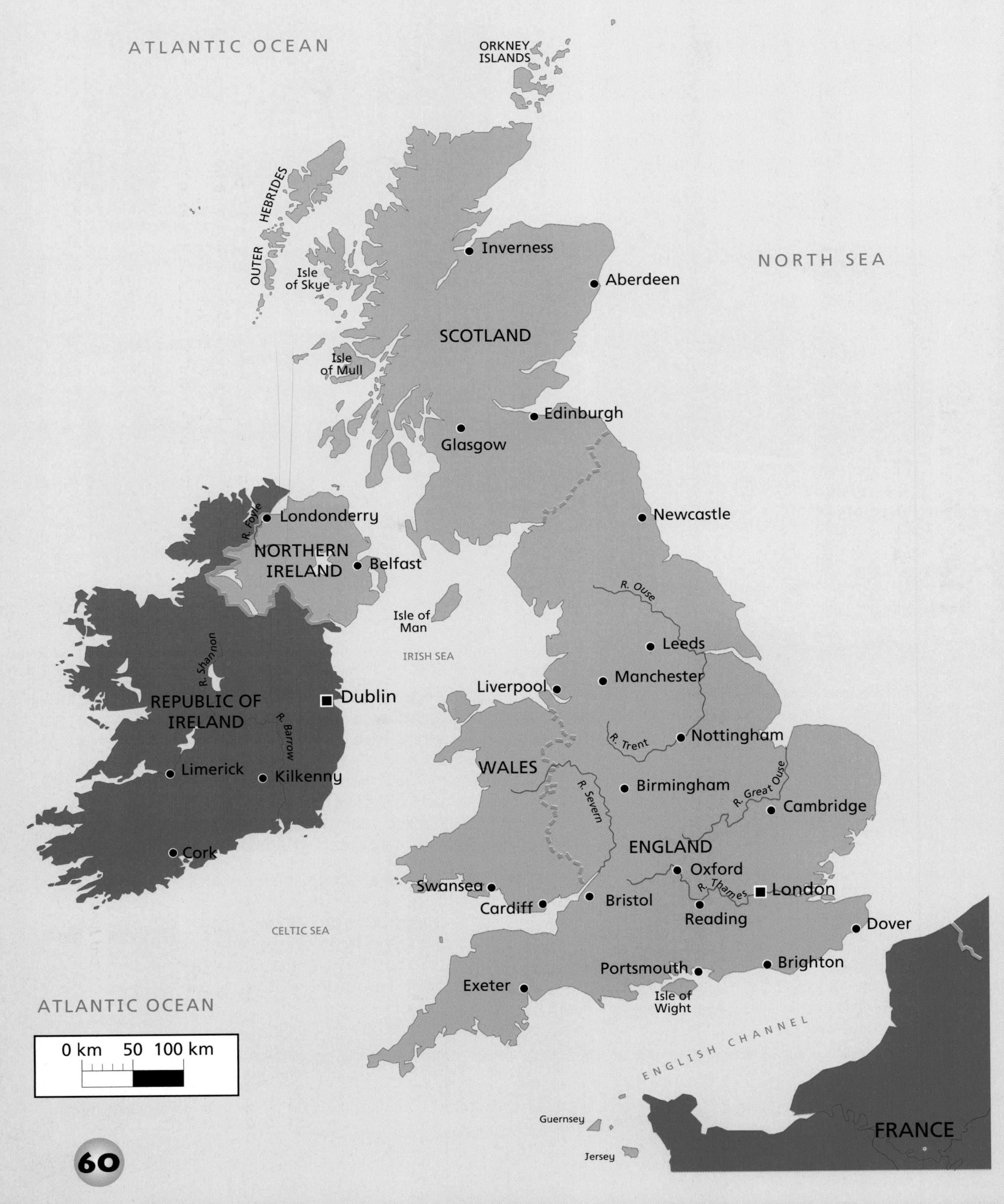

The world

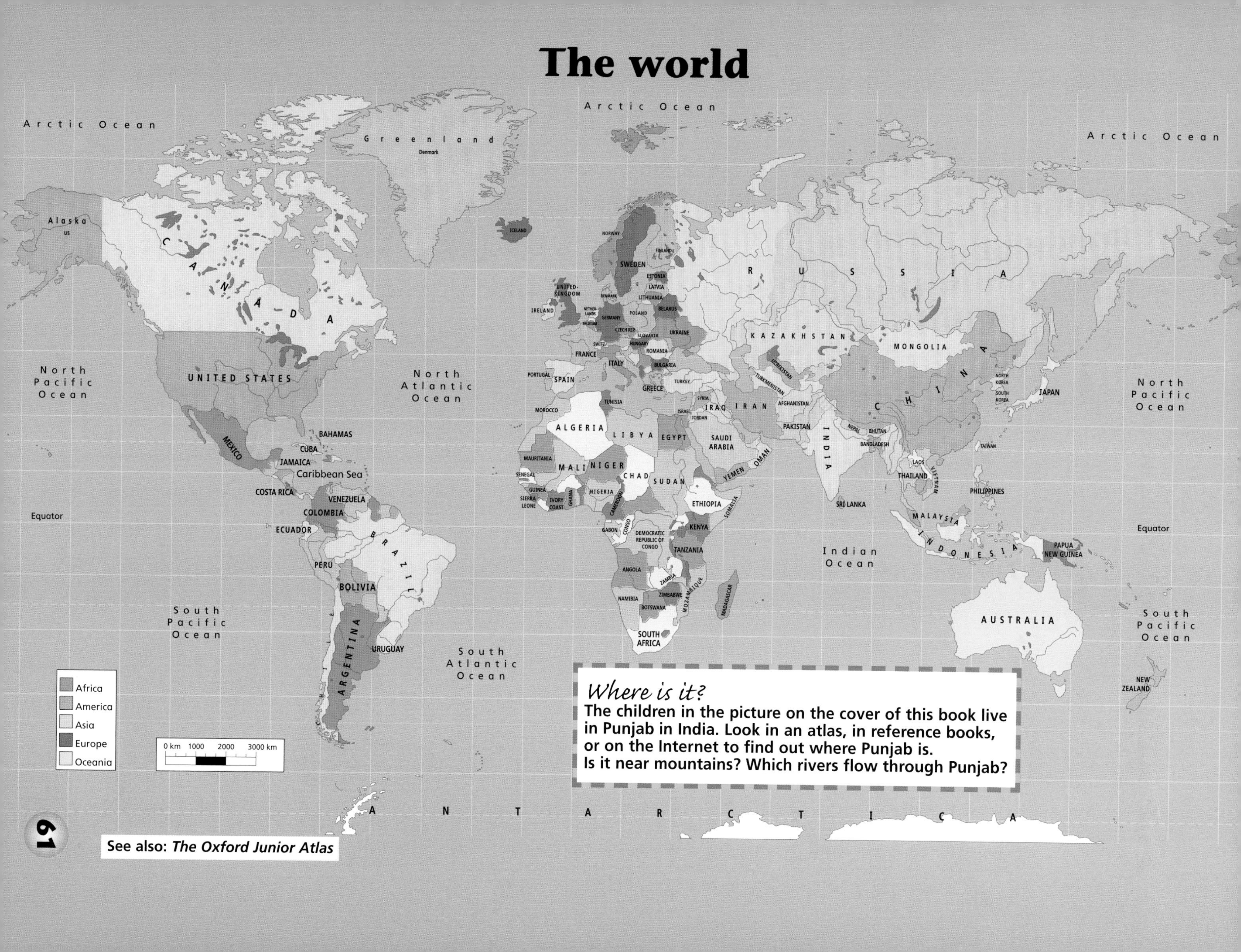

Where is it?

The children in the picture on the cover of this book live in Punjab in India. Look in an atlas, in reference books, or on the Internet to find out where Punjab is. Is it near mountains? Which rivers flow through Punjab?

See also: *The Oxford Junior Atlas*

Glossary

Acid rain Rainwater that contains acids formed from harmful gases that can kill plants and animals and damage buildings.
Affluence Being rich.
Atmosphere The thick layer of air that surrounds the Earth.
Assembly A regular meeting or a parliament.
Avalanche A sudden collapse of snow down the side of a mountain.
Bar A ridge of sand or shingle across a bay or river mouth.
Barge A long, flat-bottomed boat used mainly on rivers and canals.
Barrage A kind of dam used to hold back water.
Basin The area of land which supplies a river with water.
Block mountain A flat-topped mountain formed when a large block of land has been pushed up between two faults.
Breakwater A wall built into the sea to protect the coast or a harbour against heavy waves.
Capital city The most important city in a country.
Cargo Goods carried in a ship or aircraft.
Cash crops Crops which are produced for sale instead of for the farmer to use.
Channel A place for water to flow along.
Cliff A steep rock face, especially on the coast.
Climate The average weather in a region of the Earth throughout the year.
Colonize To become established in an area.
Communications The ways in which people travel or pass their ideas from one place to another.
Commute To travel to work, especially by car, bus or train.
Commuter Someone who regularly travels to work, especially by car, bus or train.
Condense To cool water vapour so that it turns back to liquid.
Contaminate To pollute or infect.
Contour line A line on a map joining points that are the same height above sea-level.
Conurbation Formed when a city grows and takes in surrounding towns and villages (e.g. London).
Croft A small farm in Scotland.
Crofter A farmer who farms a croft in Scotland.
Crust The Earth's outer layer of rock.
Dam A large wall or bank built to hold back water and to raise its level. A large lake called a reservoir is often formed behind a dam.
Delta An area of flat land at the mouth of a river made of mud dumped there by the river. Many deltas are shaped like a triangle.
Deposition The dropping of mud, sand and pebbles when moving water is slowed down.
Desert A dry region with very few plants.
Desertification The process in which once fertile land is turned into desert.
Developed country A rich country with modern roads, homes, schools, hospitals and factories.
Devolution The handing over of some of the powers of government to a regional assembly or parliament.
Donor A person, country or organization who gives something to someone else.
Drain To remove surplus water from a place.
Drought An unusually long period of dry weather.
Dyke An embankment.
Environment Your surroundings.
Equator An imaginary line around the centre of the Earth.
Erosion The wearing away of land by wind, moving water or ice.
Estuary The wide mouth of a river where fresh water meets the sea water.
Evaporate When water is heated it disappears into the air as water vapour. It is said to evaporate.
Famine A severe shortage of food.
Fault A large crack or break in a series of rocks. The rocks on one or both sides of the fault may slip up or down.
Favela The name given to a shanty town in Brazil.
Fertile Land that is fertile has a rich soil that produces good crops.
Flood A river floods when it flows over its banks.
Floodplain The flat area bordering a river formed from the mud deposited by the river when it floods.
Fold mountain A mountain thrown up into huge folds or ridges by movements of the Earth's plates.
Ford A shallow place where a river can be crossed.
Fuel A material that is burned to produce heat and other forms of energy.
Glacier A large river of ice which flows downhill.
Gorge A narrow valley with steep sides.
Groyne A fence built at right angles to the shore to stop the beach being washed away by the sea.
Gulley A narrow channel that carries water.
Hydro-electric power station A power station which uses the energy of running water to produce electricity.
Impermeable Describes any material that does not let liquids and gases pass through.
Irrigation Taking water from rivers, lakes, reservoirs or wells and channelling it to the land so that crops grow well.
Lagoon A shallow lake separated from the sea by a sandbank or spit.
Leeward The side that faces away from the wind.
Loch A lake in Scotland.

Longshore drift The slow shifting of sand and pebbles along a beach when waves move towards the shore at an angle.
Malnourishment Not having enough food to eat.
Mantle The layer of hot rock below the Earth's crust and above the core.
Meander A large S-shaped bend in a river.
Monsoon A wind which blows in the Indian Ocean, bringing heavy rains in the summer.
Mountain A hill that is more than 300 m high.
National park A large area of land set aside so that beautiful scenery is not spoiled, and so that rare plants and animals can be protected.
Natural gas A gas formed from the remains of tiny plants and animals that lived millions of years ago.
Nuclear fuel A fuel used in nuclear power stations to produce electricity.
Obese Used to describe someone who is very fat.
Ox-bow lake A lake made when a river changes course and cuts off a meander.
Peak The pointed top of a mountain.
Permeable Describes any material that lets liquids and gases pass through it.
Plate One of the large sections of the Earth's crust.
Plateau An area of high but flat land.
Polder Fertile land in the Netherlands that is below sea level and has been drained of water.
Pollution When substances such as air, water or soil are spoiled or made dirty by people.
Population People who live in a particular place.
Port A place where ships can be loaded or unloaded.
Pot-hole A small round hole carved in the rocky bed of a river by stones which have been swirled around by the current.
Power station A building or place where electricity is produced.
Prevailing wind The most common wind direction in a particular place.
Rain shadow The sheltered side of a mountain where there is less rainfall than on the other, windward, side.
Range A row or line of mountains.
Reef A line of rocks or coral near the sea's surface.
Refinery A place where oil is made pure.
Refugee A person who has fled from danger.
Relief map A map showing how high the different parts of a region or country are.
Reservoir A large artificial lake used to store water.
Rift valley A steep-sided valley formed when a block of land slips down between two faults.
Sand dune A hill of wind-blown sand.
Scree The bank of pieces of rock which collects at the bottom of a steep mountain slope.
Sea wall A wall made of concrete or stone built to protect beaches and buildings from the sea.
Sewage Waste materials and liquid from houses and factories, carried away by drains or sewers.
Sewer A drain that carries waste matter away.
Shanty town An area of a city where people have built their own houses from waste materials.
Siege The action of surrounding a place in order to attack it or to prevent people from leaving it.
Silt Tiny particles of rock that are smaller than sand but larger than clay.
Source The place where a river rises.
Spit A ridge of sand or shingle joined to the land at one end and sticking out into the sea at the other.
Spring The trickle of water formed when rainwater seeps out of the ground.
Surge The sudden rise in sea level when strong winds blow a high tide towards the land.
Swamp A marsh.
Terrace One of a series of level areas on a slope or hillside that looks like a huge step.
Tide The rise and fall of the oceans and seas twice a day due to the pulling effect of the Moon and Sun on the water.
Topographic map A map showing both natural features, such as hills and rivers, as well as human features, such as roads, railways and towns.
Transport [1] Buses, cars, lorries, trains and other ways of taking people or goods from one place to another. [2] The movement of eroded material by a river, the sea, a glacier or the wind.
Trawler A fishing boat that pulls a large net.
Tributary A river or stream which flows into a larger river or stream.
Upper reaches The parts of a river or canal near its beginning or source.
Valley A stretch of lower land between hills or mountains.
Volcano A hole or tear in the Earth's crust from which molten rock (lava) flows. A hill or mountain may form around this hole or tear.
Waterfall A sudden fall of water over a step or ledge in the bed of a river.
Water cycle The movement of water from the oceans, seas and other wet surfaces to the air, then back to the ground, oceans and seas again.
Water vapour The gas that forms when water is heated and evaporates.
Weather How wet, dry, hot or cold the air is at a particular time.
Weathering The breaking up of rocks by heat, cold, ice and rainwater.
Windward The side that faces the wind.

Index